SERENITY
IN WORKPLACE
CALAMITY

Identifying, Navigating and
Overcoming Workplace Bullying

CONTENTS

FOREWORD
by Lynne Curry, Ph.D., SPHR
(senior professional in human resources)

John Martz lived the workplace bullying experiences he walks his readers through. In *Serenity in Workplace Calamity,* Martz writes a personal yet educated account that will appeal to those caught in the steel web of bullying and harassment. For Martz, the bullying led to a shooting, an employee's death, and Martz's commitment to transform others' lives. The bullying impacted Martz's sense of peace, his work performance, and his pocketbook.

What makes Martz's book effective stems from his commitment to helping others facing the challenges he overcame. He intentionally establishes a one-on-one relationship with his readers and conveys, "I want to support you."

Further, Martz makes what he presents easily relatable by linking well-known movies to bullying actions from target-shaming to encroaching on employees' personal lives. This offers those humiliated by being a bully's targets the comfort of knowing how common bullying has become.

After Martz clearly defines the universe of bullying, and the related concepts of harassment and conflict, he walks readers through practical action steps readers need to take to survive and thrive.

In *Beating the Workplace Bully* (AMACOM, 2016), I let readers know that when a bully confronts you, you may wonder, "Why me?" The answer—while bullying says more about the bully than it does about you, you're the one who has to learn to stand up for yourself. Further, you can't expect a bully will go away on his or her own. Bullies perceive avoidance as an invitation to take advantage.

Those who don't stand up to the bully's initial attack signal they're easy prey and inadvertently encourage continued bullying. If you've picked up *Serenity in Workplace Calamity*, you may have already learned you can't expect to receive help from your coworkers, manager, or employer. You're the one under fire. *Serenity in Workplace Calamity* gives you a personal guide and additional tools for your overcoming bullying tool chest.

SECTION 1

IDENTIFY

CHAPTER 1

THE PROBLEM

Twenty-eight Years Ago…

On that cold Friday morning in March of 1995, I had no idea the chain of events that was to unfold that day, forever changing my workplace and career. Oddly the events of this day happened on my day off—one of the Fridays I had off on a compressed work schedule. Some would say good luck or Karma kept me from work that day—I would say it was providence. On a normal workday, I'd get up at 4:30 to get myself ready for work and get to the parking lot on time to catch my 5:25 vanpool. However, today I was able to sleep in until our two toddlers, Josiah, four years old, and Victoria, two years old, awoke. It was my turn to take care of the toddlers and get a head start on my weekend to-do list.

After they awoke, I headed down to the basement with them to put on one of their favorite VHS videos, *Beauty and the Beast*, while I worked on the broken clothes washer. I looked forward to this time as it allowed me to process many issues of the past week: work issues, upcoming work travel, my marital challenges and the upcoming March Madness college basketball tournament. Lost in my thoughts as I worked, I was surprised at how quickly the morning went. The kids were well into their second movie, and I had finished repairing the washer, run three loads of laundry, and got a workout in when my mind turned to lunch.

Shortly after bringing the kids up for lunch, the phone rang. To my surprise, it was my admin at work calling. In the six years I worked for the Department of Navy, she had never called me at home, so my mind initially turned to my current project thinking there had been an engineering issue needing to be solved. In my wildest thoughts I hadn't come close to guessing the reason for her call—the news that would change my life.

By the end of the phone call, my wife, who had been upstairs doing paperwork, had come down to join us for lunch. As I hung up the phone, my wife mirrored what must have been shock in my own face and asked in a bewildered voice, "Who was that?" So I told her it was my admin assistant from work—she had said not to come into work because there had been a shooting. She gave me no details except that it wasn't in our office and wasn't in our building. I had asked her if anyone had been killed and she had no idea. At that point, she didn't even know if the shooter was a fellow employee, contractor, or some other outside agent. She had only been instructed to call everyone not already in the office and let them know not to come in that day.

My heart sank and my mind raced that afternoon. Did anyone get hurt? Who was the shooter? And why were they shooting? All these thoughts flooded my mind as I worked through my afternoon chores.

For me, the evening news couldn't come soon enough. We didn't typically watch the evening news but tonight we would. As we tuned in, the news teased the story at the beginning of the broadcast, saying that one employee had died in a work shooting earlier that morning in one of the Department of the Navy buildings, and more details would be shared later in the broadcast. The news and commercials seemed to drag on for what seemed like hours before they got to the story, covering the weather forecast, politics, and sports before giving the full details.

When they finally shared the details, I was stunned to find out that the shooting had taken place in an office that I frequented often and even worked in. And then the bombshell—the shooter was a close colleague of mine! He had shot two other employees, both in critical condition, before turning the gun and killing himself. He was the last one I would have suspected to be the shooter as he was a calm, mild-mannered gentleman who wore a medical bracelet and reminded me of a seventy-year-old Don Knotts. A reporter interviewed his neighbors at the end of the cul-de-sac in a quiet suburb in Waldorf, Maryland. Each neighbor interviewed had the same response—they were shocked that he was the shooter as he was quiet, calm, and mild-mannered.

When I learned what office the shooting had taken place in, I knew what the likely cause was: workplace bullying. The office where the shooting occurred was led by one of the biggest workplace bullies in our organization. Having done a one-month rotation to that office a year earlier, I witnessed firsthand the tactics that this bully used: yelling, belittling, and humiliating those with opposing views. The shooter had likely internalized his emotions from years of bullying by this leader before reaching a breaking point.

The following week, I found out more of the details of the shooting. The shooter had shot the two colleagues with "birdshot", which is less lethal than other ammunition, and then loaded his gun with lethal ammunition he intended to use on the bully. Thankfully the office bully had the wherewithal to hide under his desk before the shooter entered his office, thus saving his life. Additionally, I found out that the disagreement that had gotten the shooter angry was regarding the discussion I had with him the week of the shooting.

The program office had initially agreed with our position on the project he was assigned and then later flipped. And when they flipped, the workplace bully resorted to his normal bulldozing tactics to get things his way—yelling and humiliating this older gentleman. Later in the book, I'll share how this shooting changed my career.

Because of the shooting, free counseling was offered to all employees and security was stepped up for those entering and leaving those buildings. But unfortunately, no changes were made to the work culture to prevent future bullying, and no training was given for healthy conflict resolution. In fact, the bully leader retained his position with no apparent consequences for his bullying tactics. Months later, I asked a friend who worked for the bully whether he had changed his behavior, and the friend told me that he had initially but was slipping back into his bullying tactics.

Many of my friends and family are hearing this story for the first time, as it's a memory that I've tried to suppress. In fact, I filed it so deep in my memory that I only thought to add it to the book after my first draft was complete. As you would probably guess, this story affects me to this day, twenty-eight years later.

Your Bullying or Harassment Situation: Why I Wrote This Book

I'd like to say this story is my only encounter with bullying in my thirty-four year career, but unfortunately it's not. I've observed and been on the receiving end of multiple bullying and harassment situations that have negatively impacted my peace of mind, work performance, career path, and my pocketbook to the tune of over $2 million in lost pay and benefits. Instead of letting these situations bring me down, it's fueled a passion in me to help others who find themselves in bullying or harassment situations.

When you find yourself in the middle of a bullying or harassment situation, your emotions can run the gamut as mine have in my harassment and bullying situations: anger, frustration, helplessness, and a general restlessness and unsettled feeling. You didn't ask for this person to enter your world and spill their toxicity and yet, here you find yourself. I mean seriously, work would be so much easier without these unnecessary negative interactions. You may ask yourself—should I stay or should I go? Is it my fault? How did this all start? What can I do to stop it? What are my options if I stay? Is this harassment, bullying, or general conflict?

It's funny how the mind works overtime on these questions too, whether you want it to or not and whether there's an answer or not. Not only do you think of your situation at work but on your drive home, at home when you're trying to relax, and in the middle of the night when you're trying to go back to sleep.

Unlike other situations where you can walk away if you're getting bullied or harassed, you can't completely walk away from bullying and harassment in the workplace. You can walk away from the person yelling inappropriate things from a truck as you walk by, but in the case of workplace bullying or harassment, you must return to the scene of the bullying or harassment—daily. This is the uniqueness of workplace harassment and bullying—it's inescapable. This is especially the case when your bully is a direct supervisor.

And to boot, some bullying is more covert, in more of a passive-aggressive form less detectable by the organization and even leaving you wondering yourself if you've been bullied or harassed! Covert bullying and harassment can be more damaging than more overt bullying and harassment because it's less detectable but just as harmful. In fact, there are so many covert forms of bullying and harassment that I've listed them out as A-Z in chapter 2—that's twenty-six categories! And the crazy thing is that this isn't all of them.

If you've found yourself in a similar place—asking yourself these or similar questions and having your

thoughts dominated by trying to solve these issues—
then this book is for you. My reason for writing this
book is for Y-O-U. To coach you through your situation
as one who's been through these issues in my past. My
advice comes from:

- My personal experience in identifying, navigating,
  and overcoming my bullying and harassment
  situations
- Over ten years of training and coaching leaders
  to build their organizations on the foundation
  of self-awareness and healthy conflict resolution
  skills

Through my coaching in the book, I'll help you identify
the difference between workplace bullying, workplace
harassment, and general workplace conflict. For those
conflicts that have crossed over into workplace
bullying or harassment, I'll give you the steps to
RECTIFY your situation (chapter 3), rise above your
situation, and move on, freeing yourself up to be your
productive, creative, inspired, and innovative self. And,
if it's general workplace conflict you're facing, I'll give
you the tools to get you to a win-win situation with
those who hold opposing views. This book is intended
to help you help yourself, giving strategies and
methods toward making yourself more resilient to
bullying and harassment situations. Lastly, I'll help you
become your best advocate, being more assertive in

creating a safe space by respectfully creating boundaries when encountering harassment or bullying.

I want the advice and words within these pages to help you feel:

- Empowered
- Strengthened
- At peace
- Supported

Bullying and Harassment in Society: You're Not Alone

Growing up, some of my favorite movies were those where the bullied overcame the bullies, such as in *My Bodyguard* (Bill), *The Never-Ending Story* (Petersen), or *A Christmas Story* (Clark). And there are countless high school coming-of-age movies with bullying and harassment woven throughout the plot. Unfortunately, the bullying doesn't end once you leave high school, it just enters a new realm—the workplace. Workplace bullying and harassment has fueled such movies as *Horrible Bosses*, *9 to 5*, *Anger Management*, and *Working Girl* , employing A-list actresses and actors such as Jane Fonda, Jack Nicholson, Adam Sandler, Harrison Ford, Sigourney Weaver, Dolly Parton, Melanie Griffith, Jennifer Anniston, Charlie Day, Jason

Bateman, Jason Sudeikis, Jamie Foxx and Kevin Spacey. And unfortunately, we can't ride on our magical dog dragon and escape to a magical place as Bastian did in *The Never-Ending Story* (Petersen) or hire a bodyguard to take care of our bullies as in the movie *My Bodyguard* (Bill). When I pitched this book idea to family and friends, my brother Joe (who works in Human Resources) joked: 90 percent of the work population is getting bullied and the other 10 percent are the bullies. Sadly, his figures aren't that far from the truth, as the following data from the Workplace Bullying Institute (WBI) shows (Namie):

- 49 percent of the workforce has been bullied or witnessed it (30 percent bullied & 19 percent witnessed)
- 59 percent of the workforce experienced bullying while working remotely (via group virtual meetings, private virtual meetings, group emails and private emails)

So essentially half the work population has been affected by bullying and, during lockdowns, this number increased to 60 percent! In all, the WBI estimates that 79.3 million workers in the US have been affected by bullying with 48.6 million having been bullied and 30.6 million having witnessed bullying (Namie). And I believe these numbers to be an underestimate as this survey didn't include covert forms of bullying that quite often go undetected by organizations and even the target of bullying because it is done behind closed doors or subversively.

Bullying and Harassment and Our Psyche

Within our psyches, each of us has a deep-seated desire to see justice come to those who bully, harass, or harm others, especially if we or a loved one is the one being bullied. Many books and movies leverage this desire as a way of holding the attention of the audience. Just last night I watched such a movie titled *Last Seen Alive*. In the movie a woman is kidnapped from a gas station when she and her husband pull over to get gas. As with all these types of movies, tension is created between the audience and the antagonist by showing the bad deeds of the antagonist (the kidnapper in this case) to the protagonist (the husband and wife who were minding their own business at a gas station). The worse the behavior of the antagonist, the greater the tension is created with the audience and the greater the desire of the audience to see justice come to the antagonist.

Shakespeare said, "All of the world is a stage and all of the men and women merely players." One major difference between the theater and the real world is that the theater has both protagonists and antagonists, whereas in the real world we only have protagonists. Each person, in the real world, sees themselves as the protagonist in their life story; it is the same for both the bully and the bullied. Both the bully and the bullied see themselves as protagonists in their own story from their firsthand perspective, and they see their plight as just. And seeing your bully or harasser as the protagonist in their life story can be the beginning of empathy for that person.

In the story that I shared at the beginning of this chapter, both the office bully and the shooter saw themselves as protagonists in the given situation, and each of them saw their viewpoint as the correct one. The problem started and escalated when they saw the other person as an antagonist. And so it is also for you in your situation: you need to see the other person as a protagonist, which will help you keep your focus on the issues and not the other person.

Going back to movies, books, and plays that use an antagonist and protagonist to create tension, could you imagine the heartburn you'd feel if the bad guy didn't get justice and no future book or movie was planned? You, as the protagonist in your own story, experience this every time you don't resolve the conflict in your own life. And if your personality is more of a conflict avoidance type, then you will procrastinate facing the conflict, causing you to thus internalize and build up the feelings related to bullying or harassment.

Internalizing your feelings will cause you to resent the other person(s) in each conflict and will affect you both mentally and physically.

To Your Health

So unfortunately, these situations at work can happen every day if you happen to work for this individual or work in the same building. And again, unlike other bullying situations, you are unable to get away from these individuals. I know that for me, in my situations, two of the five situations involved daily interactions with these individuals. One was a colleague in the same building as me and the other was a direct supervisor. The one who was a colleague I could avoid somewhat as he and I weren't on teams together. But in the case where the bullying was coming from my direct supervisor, there was no way out. I remember "fantasizing" about not working for this person anymore. Daily and sometimes hourly, I was looking for a way out. It was affecting my headspace at home and at work as my thoughts were dominated by trying to find some resolution to the situation. Lost sleep was an issue when I'd wake up in the middle of the night and think about the situation and not be able to get back to sleep.

When these situations occur, it can be draining on you mentally and physically. The following are some of the ways you can be affected mentally by bullying that goes unchecked:

1. Anger
2. Agitation
3. Frustration
4. Anxiety
5. Racing thoughts
6. Feeling bad about yourself (low self-esteem)
7. Overwhelmed
8. Trauma
9. Grief
10. Depression
11. Panic attack(s)
12. Post-Traumatic Stress Disorder (PTSD)

And because there is a close relationship between your mental state and physical state, a bullying situation at work can result in the following physical issues as well:

1. Insomnia
2. Nervousness or shaking
3. Headaches
4. Trouble breathing
5. Aches, pains, or tense muscles
6. Chest pain
7. Clenched jaw and grinding teeth
8. Elevated blood pressure (hypertension)

9. Gastrointestinal issues (including diarrhea, constipation, or nausea)
10. Stress-induced heart conditions
11. Panic attacks
12. Eating disorder (over- or under-eating)

The severity of these mental and physical factors will be driven by the severity, frequency, and duration of the bullying/harassment. In fact, the more covert forms of bullying/harassment can be more damaging than overt bullying because covert bullying can be equally as severe but can be more frequent and go on for a longer period of time. This happens because it's less detectable by the organization and even the individual being bullied or harassed. It's for this reason that I'll take a deeper dive into the covert forms of bullying in the next chapter.

Your Job Performance

If you're being bullied at work, your job performance will likely suffer from these negative mental and physical factors. And if your bullying situation comes from a direct supervisor, then it can also include excessive negative feedback. Without mitigation, these factors can work together in a negative feedback loop lowering your performance even further as it did for me in my bullying situation. My negative feedback loop included the following: 1) I was distracted at work and at home by trying to think of a way out, 2) I couldn't think as clearly due to lost sleep from waking up in the middle of the night thinking about the situation, and 3) negative interactions with the bully weekly and sometimes daily.

Career

One form of bullying at work that can have the largest impact on your career is calling into question your work performance through excessive negative feedback. This is one of the more impactful and more subtle forms of workplace bullying, as it can easily be passed off as "giving feedback". Most of the time we're not made aware of this form of bullying since it typically happens behind closed doors. My Human Resource representative made me aware of such a situation. She told me, "Someone in leadership is jealous of you." She didn't share the details of what the person had said nor who had said it, but she let me know that one of the leaders had said something negative about me and that it seemed unwarranted to her. When I think back on that rare insight, I think of how often this occurs without the individual being told and how easy it is for a person in a leadership position to negatively affect a person's rating for a given year or worse yet, stifle or change the course of their career.

Self-fulfilling Prophecy and Pygmalion Effect

The Pygmalion Effect is a form of the self-fulfilling prophecy where the employee will lift their performance when a supervisor's expectations are set high and lower their performance when a supervisor's expectations are set low. This effect has been shown through multiple studies in the business arena (Livingston). If you've received excessive negative feedback, it could get in your head and lower your performance. At the very least, you will find yourself having to counter the negative feedback in your mind with positive feedback you received from others. The movie *Jerry Maguire*, albeit a fictional movie, illustrates this concept. Jerry, having been one of the top employees in his field, finds himself barely holding on to one client after the negative situation of having been fired—the ultimate form of negative feedback. Throughout the movie, Jerry must counter the negativity of his situation with the positive advice from his mentor, Dicky Fox. And it will be the same for you—you will need to counter any excessive negativity with positivity.

It's a Culture Thing

If your bullying situation isn't an isolated case at your workplace, then it could be that your work environment or culture is partly to blame. A toxic work environment can foster negative work behaviors such as bullying, sabotage, or covering the truth. There's probably no better example of the repercussions of a toxic work environment than the United States Postal Service (USPS). In the late '80s and '90s, the phrase "going postal" was used to refer to any mass shooting because of the prevalence of workplace shootings that occurred at the USPS. Each of these shootings was traceable to a toxic work environment where bullying was seen as an acceptable "means to an end" where the end in this case was to have all the mail delivered without the need for overtime. I had seen this same concept of means justifying the ends firsthand when I worked in the automotive industry. I asked a team leader, who used bullying tactics regularly, why she bullied others in our team meetings, and she said, "It's always worked for me in the past." She, too, had bought into the concept of "the ends" (meeting cost and scheduling goals) justifying "the means" (her bullying tactics). She had worked through the culture of the plants that rewarded and promoted her for meeting deadlines and cost goals despite her bullying tactics. In chapter 4, I'll guide you to self-assess your work culture in helping you decide whether you should stay or go.

It's Important to Employers

Not only is it important to employees, but it's also important to employers as they want to get the most out of their workforce. And a happy workforce is a productive workforce. The corollary for this is also true. A bullied workforce is unhappy, unproductive, and likely doing the same bad behaviors or worse with their work and other employees. And if there's bullying at the top, then those directors and managers under that person may turn around and bully their own workers. Additionally, as we discussed earlier, employees who are bullied will suffer mentally and physically, so their work output is going to suffer even if they don't turn to other negative behaviors.

Fear in the Workplace

Fear in the workplace leads to multiple bad behaviors up and down the chain of command. Because of this, the management and quality guru, Dr. Edwards Deming, stated as one of his fourteen principles that organizations must identify and drive out fear. But why? For multiple reasons. For one, fear prevents the truth from being told to upper management regarding confidence in schedules, budgets, KPIs, or the viability of technical solutions. Stretching or hiding the truth can impact your organization's bottom line in the form of schedule slippage, budget overruns, inaccurate understanding of your company's health, latent product failures, or all of the above. The OceanGate submarine *Titan* implosion is an example of how organizational fear can lead a company to make bad decisions (Bogel-Burroughs, Gross and Betts). Fear in the organization prevented the engineering staff from clearly articulating the inherent safety risks of the sub. The one employee that questioned the safety of this submarine was summarily and immediately terminated and escorted from the company premises. After that, no other employee would dare make a similar stand as they would likely face the same consequences.

Additionally, your company or organization will lose productivity as an organization that lives in fear will likely be demoralized and lacking in motivation, inspiration, or creativity. So how do you identify and mitigate fear in your organization? First and foremost, your leadership team should be willing to look at your organization "in the mirror", looking at not just the good but also the blemishes. This willingness to look at your organization's blemishes then needs to be at the core of your company's philosophy and starts with confidential employee 360 reviews for each person in your organization (Dr. Lynne Curry, *Beating The Workplace Bully*). Confidential 360 reviews will help a leader see their management team from the perspective of those who work for a given manager.

This is quite often very different from the image that a manager projects to that organizational leader. Additionally, establish policies and actions that correspondingly discourage any cases of management by fear.

Fear, however, is the common reason that leaders of organizations avoid anti-bullying policies and actions, as the following common leadership team fears illustrate:

- Fear of conducting employee surveys that could reveal the prevalence of bullying and reflect poorly on the leadership team.
- Leadership not confronting bullying out of fear of negative blowback from individuals who employ bullying tactics.
- Leaders not wanting to establish anti-bullying campaigns and policies fearing that they could be accused of being bullies themselves. (Dr. Lynne Curry, *Beating The Workplace Bully*)

At the writing of this book, I'm developing organizational assessments for leaders to identify fear in their organizations, and in chapter 8, I'll highlight what leadership training can help in preventing or mitigating organizational fear.

Recap

In this chapter, I highlighted why preventing and addressing workplace bullying and harassment are important to you and your organization. In the next chapter, I'll define the differences between harassment, bullying, and general workplace conflict, which is the prerequisite to rightly navigating your situation.

I've grouped my coaching in the book into three sections that represent the three main ways I intend to help you:

- Section 1 (chapters 1 & 2) – the problem of workplace bullying and identifying whether your situation is workplace bullying, harassment, or general conflict
- Section 2 (chapters 3-5) – navigating your situation
- Section 3 (chapters 6-10) – overcoming your situation

Most of all, I want you to feel supported. As one who's been through workplace bullying and harassment myself, I know it can be a lonely and disheartening road. I want you to know that I'm here for you, and woven throughout the book is advice on how to leverage and add to your current support network, making it a less lonely road.

Chapter 1 Homework:

1. List out the twelve mental and twelve physical effects given in the book that can result from bullying or harassment:

    Mental:

    1. _____ 2. _____ 3. _____

    4. _____ 5. _____ 6. _____

    7. _____ 8. _____ 9. _____

    10. _____ 11. _____ 12. _____

    Physical:

    1. _____ 2. _____ 3. _____

    4. _____ 5. _____ 6. _____

    7. _____ 8. _____ 9. _____

    10. _____ 11. _____ 12. _____

2. For a recent bullying or harassment situation(s) at work that you've either observed or experienced, rate your emotions on a scale of one through ten, with one standing for "it didn't bother me" and ten standing for "I'm angry enough to leave my current job".

3. Write number here: _____

4. Have you had any mental or physical repercussions related to this/these incident(s)?

5. If your answer to number 3 was yes, list the ways you've been affected mentally and/or physically by this/these incident(s) using your own terms or those listed in number 1 above:

6. Extra credit: Watch any of the movies cited in this chapter and answer the following questions:

    a. Who was the antagonist?

    b. Who was the protagonist?

    c. What negative things did the antagonist do to the protagonist?

    d. How did you feel after the antagonist did these things to the protagonist?

It's important for you to address and resolve these issues now. Your future mental and physical well-being depend on it.

CHAPTER 2

BULLYING VS. HARASSMENT VS. GENERAL CONFLICT

Ask yourself: Is my situation workplace bullying, harassment, or general conflict? The answer to this question is key to knowing what path to take to bring resolution to your given workplace situation. The path for resolution for workplace bullying or harassment is in chapter 3 of this book, and the path for resolution of general workplace conflict is introduced in chapter 5. Additionally, identifying your situation as workplace bullying or harassment can be empowering in that it can validate the negative feelings you have for the person using bullying or harassment tactics.

Meeting with an Admiral

As I walked past the smells of the underground shops, my thoughts drifted between what I wanted for lunch and pondering the reason for this meeting. The meeting was set up by an admiral whom I had never met, and the subject of the meeting remained a mystery, as his meeting invite didn't specify. In the three years of working in the Department of Navy, I had run into admirals before but never had a one-on-one meeting with one.

As I rounded the corner, I came to the building where we were to meet. On the elevator ride up, I asked myself: What did this guy want? And why did he schedule this meeting? As I entered the lobby to his office, I was greeted by the admiral's admin assistant, a kind, professional woman. After letting her know who I was, she kindly asked me to have a seat. As I sat, I thought how this area reminded me of the waiting area of a doctor's office: I picked up and started flipping through one of the magazines in front of me, pretending to be to be reading but in reality, listening to the two men in the office adjacent to the lobby. I could hear that the men were having a friendly exchange. I thought that maybe my conversation would go similarly. Suddenly the men's voices got louder as they apparently moved closer to the door. As the door opened, I could see both men were wearing their white Navy uniforms. One departed with a handshake and the other retreated back to the office. Shortly after, the lady at the desk announced, "You can go in now." As I went in, the admiral, who was sitting at his desk, started the conversation off in a regular voice.

"I wanted to talk to you about your evaluation of the XYZ project."

I said, "Okay." I now knew the answer to why I was here. He wanted to talk to me about my evaluation of three potential suppliers. My mind drifted back to the testing I had conducted between three potential suppliers of a device we wanted to purchase off the shelf. I, as one of ten people in charge of evaluating these suppliers, had written an internal memo to the other team members saying that two of the three suppliers should be disqualified due to failing the test I had conducted.

The admiral then said, "I would like for you to withdraw your recommendation to eliminate two suppliers."

My response was calm and respectful. "Two of the suppliers didn't meet the requirement, so they shouldn't even be considered."

At this point the admiral stood to his feet and began to raise his voice. At first it was only mild, but as he saw that I wasn't going to change my mind, he began to berate and humiliate me using every possible curse word that came to his mind. I calmly and quietly took his yelling and cursing for the next half hour to an hour. At the end of which, I calmly stated, "I'm not changing my mind."

This story happened roughly thirty years ago. As a young twenty-five-year-old engineer, I took it on the chin. Which is probably another reason why the admiral went ballistic—he saw that he wasn't getting a reaction out of me. I bring up this story at the definition section of this book to say that this was, and it wasn't, workplace bullying. It was, because the admiral was being a bully in the moment. He had rank over me, and he had cursed a string of profanities from the east coast to the west coast...but for me, it wasn't bullying. The following details from this incident keep me from calling it workplace bullying:

1. After this meeting, I never talked to this admiral again and therefore had no additional negative interactions like the one in the story.
2. His anger and cursing hadn't affected me negatively. In my case, I brushed off what had just happened and moved on.
3. Lastly, this interaction and the results from this situation didn't impact my performance rating or career path. The manager of my department later got an email from this admiral saying that I was kicked off the team—which my manager dismissed and even took my side on the matter.

So now is a good place to introduce some definitions.

Workplace Bullying vs. Harassment vs. General Conflict

Workplace Bullying

By my definition, workplace bullying is defined by the following criteria:

1. Intentional or unintentional behavior that intimidates, humiliates, or harms another person.
2. The harm can be physical, emotional, job performance rating, or career-impacting.
3. It is repeated OR it was a one-time significant event.
4. This is done by someone in a higher position than the person being bullied (i.e., the target).

Going back to my story that I led the chapter off with, my situation with this admiral met the criteria of 1 and 4 but not 2 or 3. So by my definition, my situation with this admiral didn't meet the definition of workplace bullying. Note that #2 is in the eyes of the beholder. Someone else in the same situation could have been emotionally harmed by thirty minutes of expletives and yelling. This is why documenting how it impacted you personally is so important, as I'll detail in the next chapter.

I'm defining these up front just so we (you, the reader, and me) have a common lexicon for what I'm referring to when I say "workplace bullying". I can say with some confidence that there was likely someone else who had to deal with this admiral on a daily or weekly basis who was likely getting bullied. Culturally, bullying is a common tactic applied by enlisted servicemen and women to other enlisted servicemen or women to establish a chain of command and establish an adherence to rules and a code of conduct. Some branches being worse than others. And, as in both my chapter 1 and 2 stories, this sometimes spills over into the civilian side of these organizations.

I personally added both job performance rating and career impacting to my definition of bullying because in the workplace, career limitations could be the largest harm in each situation. Going back to my story with the admiral, had my boss taken the admiral's "kicking me off the team" seriously and let it impact my job performance rating at the end of the year or my career path, then this situation would have met criteria 2 under my definition of workplace bullying, since it would have impacted me professionally.

Note that I say workplace bullying can be intentional or unintentional. I believe that there are some individuals who gravitate toward bullying behavior because they do it so often, it's become a habit. And as a habit, they're not self-aware enough to know when they're doing it. They've done it so often that it's literally become part of who they are. To illustrate how this could happen, I'll refer to a work friend who always inserted the catch phrase "you know what I'm saying" at the end of what he said. A few times after he said that I would say, "No, I don't know what you're saying." He would then look at me quizzically as if to say, "Why did you say that?" He had inserted this phrase so many times that he had no idea he had said his catch phrase. And so it is with some bullies, their bullying tactics have become such a habit for them that they're not self-aware when they're doing it.

Workplace Harassment

Workplace harassment is very similar to workplace bullying, except it's done by someone at or below your level in the workplace. Workplace harassment is, by my definition:

1. Intentional or unintentional behavior that intimidates, humiliates, or harms another person.
2. The harm can be physical, emotional, job performance rating, or career-impacting.
3. It is repeated OR it is a one-time significant event.
4. This is done by someone at the same level as yourself or someone below you.

So basically, workplace harassment is like workplace bullying in that it includes elements 1-3 that bullying has but differs from bullying in that it is done by someone at or below your level.

Workplace Conflict

I'd say that over 99 percent of my work conflict is the result of "general workplace conflict" and not workplace bullying or workplace harassment. I think this value changes significantly from person to person as there are many factors that determine the amount of harassment and bullying that an individual experiences (for example, sex, race, organizational role).

Accordingly, general workplace conflict is, simply:

- Any conflict at work that doesn't meet the criteria for workplace bullying or workplace harassment.

Elaborating further, general workplace conflict is:

1. Any situation in which two or more people have differing opinions or goals creates tension or disagreement.
2. Conflict can arise from a variety of sources, including differences in personality, communication styles, work habits, priorities, hidden agendas, or jealousy, to name just a few.

Sometimes something that is initially workplace conflict can morph into workplace harassment or workplace bullying.

Unlike workplace bullying or harassment, workplace conflict is not necessarily one-sided, and it does not necessarily involve a power dynamic.

Am I Experiencing Workplace Bullying? Harassment?

I'm sure this is a question at the forefront of your mind since you're reading this book. I remember one of my situations where I thought I might be experiencing workplace bullying; a close work confidant shared a bullying survey. I wasn't quite certain if it was just general work conflict that was the result of personality and priority differences or if it was truly workplace bullying because a lot of what had been said wasn't overtly bad. So when I finished the survey and the survey said that yes, I was experiencing workplace bullying, I felt validated. It helped to validate the daily feeling of dread I experienced whenever I had to meet with this individual and my desire to work someplace else doing anything else. Prior to working for this person, I loved my job and loved what I did. While working for this individual, I fantasized daily and sometimes hourly about leaving. I took this survey before I had put some thought into my bullying and harassment definitions. And so, I just now scrolled back up in my current draft of this book to see if my situation met my four criteria for workplace bullying and yes it did, as I'll list out here:

1. Intentional or unintentional behavior that intimidates, humiliates, or harms another person - yes.
2. The harm can be physical, emotional, job performance rating, or career-impacting - yes.
3. It is repeated over a period of time OR it was a significant event that happened only once - yes.
4. This is done by someone in a higher position than the person being bullied - yes.

Why were my answers for each of the above "yes"?

For number 1, I include both "intentional or unintentional" because in many cases, you won't be able to tell whether the individual bullying you is meaning to do it and you will likely not know why. This allows you to self-evaluate. For my situation, I didn't know if my boss was intending to do what they were doing and I didn't know why they were doing it (although I suspected that it was driven by differences in goals, priorities, and our personalities). But the beauty of numbers 1 and 2 coupled together is that it is in the eyes of Y-O-U. If you feel like you're being affected emotionally or job performance-wise or career-wise, then it meets the criteria of numbers 1 and 2 above.

Number 3 is met if it's repeated behavior that keeps you wondering, "What is it going to be today," or if you're dreading going to a one-on-one meeting with this individual because something might be said or done that ruins your day or week. I added a one-time event as a possible criteria for meeting number 3 in the definition because some events are bad enough to be to be classified as bullying—if the event was your work termination, a negative end-of-year performance evaluation or overt sexual harassment, then that one-time event is enough to meet the criteria of number 3 above. And I can put "yes" for number 4 above because, in my situation, it was my direct supervisor who was doing the bullying.

You also can quickly surmise whether what you're experiencing is workplace bullying or workplace harassment in accordance with my definitions. Simply ask yourself if each of the four criteria applies to your specific situation. If you answer yes to all four, then you're experiencing bullying/harassment in the workplace.

To determine the degree of your bullying or harassment situation, I've developed a bullying survey to help you know whether you're being bullied and to what degree. At the time of the writing of this book, I intend to make it available for free to everyone, either sending it out to you via email or the web.

Types of Bullies. I've divided the types of bullies into two major categories: overt and covert. The overt bullies are more easily detected by both the organization and the individual being bullied. The admiral in the lead-off story to this chapter was displaying overt behavior: raising his voice and cursing a string of obscenities for a half hour to an hour. And anyone listening would have thought the same. On the other hand, the covert type of bullying is more difficult to detect by both the organization and the employee being bullied. If you're being bullied by a covert bully, then you're feeling the stress from this bully weekly, daily, and possibly hourly but not able to point to a specific overt action that would require a Human Resource representative to get involved. Overt bullying includes yelling, cursing, humiliating, inappropriate touching, or overt forms of sexual harassment.

The A-Z of Covert Bullying or Harassment

I specifically list out the covert forms of bullying or harassment because they are not as obvious to the casual observer. Most of these apply to both bullying as well as harassment with the difference being that bullying will be coming from someone above your level and harassment will come from someone at or below your level. The following are the major forms of covert bullying and harassment:

a. **Covert task micromanagement**. Task micromanagement would be the micromanaging of your day-to-day activities. Wanting to see and approve of every communication, presentation, or analysis that you perform. If you're early in your career you may need, welcome, or even ask for this type of feedback. But if you've been well established in your career (three-plus years) and someone at your immediate supervisor's level or above is asking to have detailed involvement in your daily tasks, then you're experiencing covert task micromanagement.

b. **Covert time micromanagement**. If someone is asking for an accounting of your time or regularly drops hints wanting to know your whereabouts, then you could be experiencing covert time micromanagement. When I worked in the automotive industry, I had a friend whose boss would text him regularly, asking where he was. Sometimes he'd be in the bathroom, test lab, or at a meeting when he'd get these messages. Strict time management may be key in some jobs, such as those in the service industry or playing a key role on a production or assembly line where you're working a job that uses a time clock to punch in and out and you have scheduled breaks and a scheduled lunchtime. So the context of your type of work is important in this case. In the case of my friend, he was a salaried professional engineer, so how he was being treated by his boss's extreme time management was different than the rest of the engineers and different than how he had been treated in the past. Similarly, a non-boss could also covertly harass you in this manner; for instance, by asking for an accounting of your time: asking your whereabouts at lunchtime, when you take your lunchtime, making comments about bathroom breaks, etc. *Curb Your Enthusiasm* did a funny skit referring to the admin who sat next to the bathroom as the "the bathroom monitor". This person's monitoring of Larry David's bathroom visits would fall into this category of covert time micromanagement.

c. **Gaslighting** (in the traditional sense). The term "gaslighting" originates from the 1938 British play, *Gas Light*, which inspired several follow-up plays and movies (e.g., *Gaslight* the movie released in 1940 and again in 1944). In the movie, a husband slowly adjusts the brightness of the gas lights in their home from night to night. The woman notices this difference and begins to think she's crazy as the husband doesn't admit to changing the setting of the gas lights. A manager or fellow employee may use similar techniques to this to manipulate an employee into questioning their own perceptions, memory, or judgment regarding themselves or details of work events or interactions.

d. **Withholding positive feedback and recognition**. If you never hear any positive feedback from your immediate supervisor, it could be that the person really isn't good at giving compliments. But if you hear your immediate supervisor freely giving others recognition but never giving any to you, especially after good performance on a given task, then you are likely experiencing this form of bullying. It also could be that the other employee has a more similar personality or more similar priorities to your manager than you do.

e. **Excessive negative feedback**. If your supervisor or someone else in a leadership position is nitpicking your work and looking for something negative to say, then you are likely getting this form of negative treatment.

f. **Underrepresenting the positive work of the employee to others**. This can be done officially (e.g., through end-of-year evaluations or "talent summits") or unofficially. This could be in the form of a fallacy argument of what is called a "straw man", where the person giving the feedback on your performance misrepresents or underrepresents your work, and then that misrepresentation or underrepresentation is criticized. This type of logical fallacy is called a "straw man" argument. And it's called a straw man because it's a false representation of reality that's easy to knock down—as easy to knock down as a straw man. In this case, the misrepresentation of your work is easily criticized or "knocked over". Unfortunately, this type of feedback is typically done when you're not present. Because it's done behind closed doors, it's unlikely that it'll get back to you. You will typically only see or feel the repercussions of this type of covert bullying when the end-of-year evaluation comes up and you get a negative rating, or you're held in your position or you find yourself as one of the few selected for termination in a layoff. In chapter 1, I shared that my Human Resource representative said a senior manager was jealous of me. This senior manager was using a straw man argument where he misrepresented my work and then easily "knocked it over" during a "talent summit".

g. **Giving more work to one employee over others**. If you're getting more work than others working in your group, it could be because they see you as a harder worker and thus able to handle more work, OR they are simply not being fair in the allotment of work. If your workload is higher than a fellow worker AND the other employee is getting more positive feedback, then you are likely to experience this form of bullying or harassment. This type of bullying could be used to set the target up for failure, missing deadlines, or expectations.

h. **Having higher expectations for you over other employees in your group**. In this form of covert bullying, you're being held to a different standard than other employees in your group. It is possible that you're getting different treatment because your role within the group is different. For example, an administrative assistant vs. the engineers in the group will have differing roles and responsibilities and therefore there will be differing expectations. Additionally, someone with more experience and higher pay is going to have higher expectations placed on them than an early career individual with lower pay.

i. **Sabotaging an employee's work**. Sabotage in the work environment is deliberately destroying, damaging, obstructing, or misdirecting someone else's work. In the work environment, sabotage could be done in so many ways: by undoing your work, by changing something that you've done, by accessing your email and sending out an email or message to someone else from your computer or deleting something you've sent from someone else's computer.

j. **Trapping you physically**. This could be someone standing in a doorway and not allowing you to get out of a room, pulling behind your car in a parking lot when you're ready to back out, or sneaking up behind you and pinning your head to a desk. Believe it or not, the latter two have happened to me in my professional engineering work environments.

k. **Trapping you positionally**. This is more easily done by a direct supervisor by giving you negative ratings or simply holding you back from a promotion as was done in the movie *Horrible Bosses* to Justin Bateman's character, Nick Hendricks, by his boss, Dave Harken, portrayed by Kevin Spacey. In the movie *9 to 5*, the character Franklin Hart did this to Violet Newstead (Lily Tomlin's character) when he chooses to promote a man that works for Violet over the ultra-responsible Violet. This could also be done by a non-supervisor who speaks to someone about a position that you apply for by asking them to remove you from consideration for a job that could be a promotion for you. Or it could be done more subtly by misrepresenting your contribution and work to the hiring manager for a position that you've applied for.

l. **Treating you differently from others in your group**. This can show up in so many ways, some of which I've already mentioned, such as the amount of work or feedback. These methods could be more subtle, such as not getting to speak in meetings, getting more negative feedback, or getting less respect. This could happen in any way that makes you feel different than the others in your group.

m. **Social isolation**. Not inviting you to team gatherings such as a team meeting, a team holiday gathering, team luncheon, or a team celebration. This could be an oversight by the planner of the meeting, or it could be a form of social isolation. It becomes more obvious and less likely to be just happenstance if it happens multiple times. This could also show up in the form of the person continually canceling meetings with you.

n. **Favoritism or nepotism**. This is typically shown by someone in a higher position. Allowing favorites to have special favors, promotions, travel, or other perks or favors.

o. **Encroaching on life outside of work**. This could be in the form of phone calls or text messages outside of business hours or over weekends. Again, the context of your work comes into play in determining whether this is covert bullying. If you're a line worker or in the service industry, then your work ends when you clock out, and you shouldn't be getting calls or text messages outside of work. If you're a salaried employee whose job is to keep a production line up and running, then getting phone calls or text messages outside of work hours is expected. Or you're a salaried employee and you must work past typical work hours or over the weekends to get a special project done, travel for work or otherwise. In these cases, communication with a boss or other employee on those occasions would be expected. This would be considered bullying or harassment if there's an inordinate amount of work or communications outside of work or the communications are nonwork-related.

p. **Shaming and belittling**. This can occur in a one-on-one situation or in front of others. If you or your work is shamed or belittled, then you are likely experiencing this form of bullying or harassment. This will obviously be more hurtful if done in front of others and will hurt more if it's an attack on your character or who you are. If they are shaming or belittling you for who you are, then it's crossed over into being overt harassment or bullying.

q. **Dropping random negative comments**. I call this "death by a thousand pinpricks". Just one pinprick isn't going to hurt. But if it's done incessantly, then you're experiencing this form of bullying and harassment. Think of it this way—one bee or wasp sting is going to hurt but not be lethal. But getting stung over and over by aggressive bees, wasps, or hornets could literally kill you. You could also analogize this to a dripping faucet. Just one drop isn't going to bother you. But a continual dripping faucet is. Over time these negative comments add up to something significant that is going to bother even the most resilient person.

r. **Prohibiting access to necessities**. This could be prohibiting you from getting adequate bathroom breaks, lunchtime breaks, or just a quick break to reset your mind.

s. **Any kind of touching**. This includes any and every form of touching—in the United States, any touching outside of a handshake is off-limits. Rubbing someone's shoulders, hugging, or brushing against someone else are unacceptable forms of touching.

t. **Respect the bubble**. In the US, social distance with colleagues is from two to four feet. Obviously during Covid, that increased to six feet. In any case, others with whom you work should respect your social bubble and not encroach on that. Obviously, there are social situations where this doesn't apply such as flying in an airplane or riding in an elevator.

u. **Withholding key information necessary to perform your job**. In this form of bullying or harassment, your boss or someone you work with is withholding key information for you to do your job. This could also be done by a coworker withholding key information necessary for you to perform a task, meet their or someone else's expectations, or improve your personal work performance. One example of this that happened to me was when a supervisor told me that someone gave negative feedback about me at a "talent summit" but wouldn't tell me who it was and wouldn't tell me what they had said. So unfortunately, I couldn't speak to the person directly to understand what their issue was and address it face-to-face. In this type of covert harassment or bullying, the persons "in the know" can use this as a power play against the person "in the dark" as an advanced form of gossiping or to keep someone from fully completing their job.

v. **Falsely blame**. This occurs when you're wrongly blamed for a mistake of someone else. This is more commonly used by someone in a higher position to deflect blame from themselves when something goes wrong.

w. **Gossiping about you**. This could be something that's true or untrue about you and it can be done just as easily by someone above, at the same level, or below you. Gossiping is typically something that brings down the person being gossiped about. In the movie *9 to 5*, the character Franklin Hart gossiped about Doralee Rhodes (Dolly Parton's character) by falsely spreading rumors that he and Doralee were having an affair.

x. **Verbal intimidation**. Raising voice or using expletives with the intent of forcing others to change their opinions, goals, objectives, or work priorities. This was the methodology used by the bully in the example at the beginning of this book.

y. **Positional intimidation**. Using higher a position to intimidate others through direct threats regarding a lower performance rating, holding them back from promotions, or firing them. This can be done more subtly to others in an organization by giving lower ratings, holding back, or firing organizational foes.

z. **Intellectual intimidation**. Using knowledge of a certain subject with the intent of making the target feel inferior. As with other forms of intimidation, the reason for this form of intimidation is to change another person's opinion, goals, priorities, or objectives.

Sadly, this list doesn't cover every form of covert harassment or bullying, but it gives you an idea of the sheer number of ways that covert bullying and harassment can take place. One of the key factors in these types of bullying or harassment is what is the intent of the bully or harasser? Does the bully or harasser's behavior seem intentional? You will know this from the frequency and severity of each of these types of covert behaviors. You will also be able to pick up on intent from the nonverbal cues—their attitude toward you vs. others and their body language and facial expressions when talking to you.

Many of these covert forms of bullying or harassment are used because they'll go undetected by the organization and possibly go undetected by the person being bullied. Unfortunately, those who employ this form of bullying have learned to do so skillfully or in a manner that they've gotten away with in the past, therefore emboldening them to do it in the future. They could "sell" their tactics to others as just giving feedback. I'll delve into your options for resolving this type of behavior in the next chapter. Quite often this form of bullying is done by someone above you and done behind closed doors, so you won't know that it's occurring necessarily. You will simply feel the repercussions of it. Some of these forms of bullying or harassment are more severe than others. The more severe forms are typically more noticeable but not necessarily.

Bully Boss vs. Good Manager/Leader

If you feel dread going to one-on-one meetings or running into your boss in the hallways or your anxiety level is off the charts regarding any sort of work that's going to require involvement from your immediate supervisor, then you could be experiencing bullying. A good manager will give you feedback with the intent of helping you improve yourself or your work. Whereas a bully will use more passive-aggressive techniques that would follow one or more of the covert tactics I brought up in my A-Z list. If I were to look at all of the managers in the world, they would have a hybrid combination at and between the following traits for a The Bully Boss vs. The Good Manager/Leader:

The Bully Boss	The Good Manager/Leader
Micromanages tasks	Empowers and trusts you to do your work
Brings you down	Inspires you to be your best self and do your best work
Criticizes you	Offers constructive criticism toward helping you improve
Rarely, if at all, gives positive feedback	Gives genuine credit when credit is due
Speaks negatively of you to others	Speaks of you positively and even promotes you
Dumps work on you	Allocates work fairly among the group
Treats you as subservient to them	Doesn't ask for you to do anything they wouldn't do
Micromanages time	Rarely asks your whereabouts
Blames you or others when things go wrong	Takes responsibility when things go wrong
Others get special treatments that you do not	Attempts to be equitable with everyone in group
Vents emotions on others	Is calm even in difficult situations

If you've had an immediate supervisor who leans toward the Good Manager/Leader, you relish those times and look back at those times with fond memories. Whereas if you've worked for an individual who leans more toward the Bully Boss, you're glad those days are over and hope that you never work for someone like that again.

Bullying vs. Constructive Feedback

Feedback is a constructive criticism or an evaluation of an employee's performance, behavior, or work. It is usually given with the intent of improving the employee's skills or work output. When feedback is constructive, it is specific, actionable, and focused on behaviors or actions that can be changed or improved.

Bullying, on the other hand, involves a boss who uses intimidation, coercion, or verbal abuse to control or manipulate an employee. It is not focused on improving performance or productivity, but on exerting power and control over the employee. The following are some key differences between feedback and bullying from a boss:

1. Intent: Feedback is given with the intention of helping the employee improve, while bullying is meant to intimidate and control the employee.

2. Tone: Feedback is given in a respectful and professional tone, while bullying is often delivered in an angry or aggressive tone.

3. Focus: Feedback is focused on specific behaviors or actions that can be improved, while bullying is focused on the employee as a person and may involve personal attacks.

4. Frequency: Feedback is typically given on a regular basis, while bullying may be sporadic or unpredictable.

5. Impact: Feedback can have a positive impact on the employee's performance and job satisfaction, while bullying can have a negative impact on the employee's mental health and overall well-being.

In summary, while feedback and bullying from a boss may both involve criticism or evaluation of an employee's performance, they are fundamentally different in their intent, tone, focus, frequency, and impact. You also will notice a difference in how you feel after constructive criticism vs. bullying. After constructive criticism, you feel motivated and energized to do better. After bullying, you feel frustrated, depressed, or angry.

Chapter 2 Homework

1. Evaluate a current or past situation of workplace conflict that you've experienced or observed by answering yes or no to each of the following criteria:

a. Intentional or unintentional behavior that intimidates, humiliates, or harms another person.

b. The harm can be physical, emotional, job performance rating, or career-impacting.

c. It is repeated OR it was a one-time significant event.

If you answer yes to all three of the above, then what you've experienced or observed is workplace bullying or harassment. By my definitions, it's workplace bullying if this is done by someone above, and if it's done by someone at or below the target, it's workplace harassment.

2. Review the list of the forms of covert bullying and list out those that you have experienced in your past.

SECTION 2

NAVIGATE

CHAPTER 3

RECTIFY

Key Steps for Navigating Bullying and Harassment

Note: This chapter is written in the context of bullying or harassment in the workplace environment. If you, your children, or someone close to you experiences bullying or harassment in school, online, or some other venue, you can follow these exact same steps. The only difference will be that you will be appealing to a different authority than a supervisor in the "Talk" step. For example, in a school bullying situation you would appeal to the schoolteachers, counselors, and principal instead of your immediate supervisor and Human Resource representative, and in the online bullying scenario, you would talk to the website administrator or mediator.

I like to use acronyms and acrostics because they're an easy way to remember the key steps to take in what otherwise might be a complex situation. So I've developed the acronym RECTIFY for the steps you should take if you find yourself in a bullying or harassment situation. RECTIFY stands for:

1. Record
2. Evaluate
3. Cope
4. Talk
5. Intermediary
6. File
7. beYond

You likely won't go through all these steps with each bullying or harassment event. In much of my harassment or bullying situations, I didn't go past step 5. I'll now go through the specific actions associated with each step.

Record.

Record the incident—write down the date, time, incident details, who said what, who may have observed, and don't forget to write down how it makes you feel and how it's affecting your health and work motivation. You may have been like me and not started writing down what happened at the time of the first incident. If the harassment or bullying scenario is more covert in nature, then it won't be a problem until it is. Sometimes you won't feel it's a problem until there have been several incidents. If this is the case, you will have to recall and document past incidents as well as the most recent one that was the trigger for you to start writing them down. In these cases, you'll want to write down the date that you're recalling those past incidents and the date or approximate date that the past incidents occurred, and put yourself into the mind frame and emotions immediately following those incidents to document how each of those incidents of the past made you feel. By recording this, it can be helpful both emotionally and in identifying whether it meets the definition of workplace bullying or harassment.

I have one personal case where what I would classify as "workplace conflict" turned into "workplace harassment". By way of a background, as I stated previously, I basically work with engineers and their managers. Some of us engineers lack social skills; some more so than others. One such engineer was inappropriate not just to me but to several other engineers. At some point, the things that he said and did to me got to be too much and were starting to affect my work, so I took the time to record the most recent incident and all of the previous incidents that I could remember. For each incident, I wrote down the details of what happened and the date (or approximate date it happened if it occurred in the past). In this case, this individual's office moved to another building shortly after I started to journal regarding him, so I saved it as a file on my computer thinking I could bring it back up if he moved back to my building or if anything else happened with him. Documenting it helped me to see that it was a trend and helped me later when I needed to address his behavior with my manager and Human Resource representative after his latest episode of harassment. And so it will be the same for you. It will: 1) help you to see the extent and severity of the harassment or bullying, and 2) help you to keep an accurate record of the harasser's or bully's behavior for any future actions.

Evaluate.

Evaluating your situation can help you put numbers to how your situation is affecting you mentally and your work motivation. Additionally, you can also evaluate your bully or harasser to help you better understand the contributing factors to your situation. Lastly, you should evaluate your workplace toward helping you understand if your situation is unique or it's part of a systemic issue originating from a negative workplace environment.

Bully Assessment.

Take a bully assessment to see whether your situation is a bullying or harassment situation. In the last chapter I had you assess your situation with the four elements of my bullying definition. Taking a bully assessment will add more clarity to your specific situation and assign a numerical value for the degree that your situation is affecting your mental state and your work. This numerical value can also help validate your feelings, supporting that what you've been feeling is actual harassment or bullying. Lastly, taking such a survey can support your case when sharing it with others in your organization who have the power to help you.

A bullying survey is analogous to rating your pain level on a ten-point scale when seeing a doctor, where a one is no pain at all and a ten is the most severe excruciating pain. For your bullying situation, is it a one (meaning that it's no big deal right now), is it a ten (meaning I dread seeing my bully/harasser and spend every minute of every day thinking how I can get another job internally or externally), or is it somewhere in between? My guess is that since you're reading this book, you are close to a ten already. On a ten-point scale, what is your current bullying level?

Write it here:

Is it bad enough that you want to leave? If so, you should develop an initial pros and cons list for staying vs. going. It may seem like we're locked in our situation when we aren't. Are there similar positions in the company? Look at the needs of the company and create a new role to meet that need. I did this fifteen years ago when I worked for a supervisor who had an anger problem. He would get so angry that foam would form at the corners of his mouth. So I developed a presentation for a real need in the company, and three months later I was promoted to work in a role directly for my director. And three months after that I was asked to lead the Reliability and Robustness engineering program, which was one of the best roles of my career. So it is possible to live your best work life in your current organization. It's important to self-rate your situation at a regular cadence to self-monitor whether it's getting worse.

Mental Assessment for You.

It's important to take a mental assessment to rightly understand the impact your situation is having on your mental state. Going back to chapter 1, these situations can affect your mental headspace significantly. Take such an assessment at a monthly cadence to monitor whether your mental state is getting worse, staying the same, or improving.

Personality Assessment for You.

Such an assessment can give you more insight into yourself and your personal preferences. These insights can help you understand personality types that will work well with others who will not. And it will give insight into the types of issues that can arise when working with or for someone with an opposite personality. For instance, it can show the potential issues that can arise from a detail-oriented person working for a visionary person or vice versa.

Evaluate Your Work Performance.

Does your boss's feedback seem off from feedback you've received in your past? Being in your own skin makes it difficult to get outside yourself and observe how you're perceived by others. So getting multiple outside opinions of your work can be helpful. When I thought I was in a bullying situation, I had had thirty years of experience as an engineer with a total of twenty-five bosses and never had a rating below a "meets expectations" and several "exceeds" and "outstanding" ratings. So when my performance suddenly dropped and it all started with my new boss, it was easy to see a cause-and-effect relationship. My work didn't suddenly plummet after thirty successful years. Additionally, I had eight years under my belt in my current position—all with positive ratings and no negative feedback. In fact, my previous boss and my Human Resource representative had all positive things to say about my work output and what the program was able to achieve in those eight years.

Evaluate Your Bully.

How is your bully bullying you, and why do you think your bully is bullying you? This can be empowering for you, and it can help you to get outside of yourself by seeing things from their viewpoint. Seeing your bully as being driven by their human habits, what's worked for them before, what they've gotten away with, etc. can give you the right state of mind when following the additional steps in RECTIFY. If your bully is a direct supervisor, then assessing how your bully stacks up to your direct supervisors of your past can help you to further see how your current situation is impacting you.

Evaluate Your Work Culture.

As I brought up in chapter 1, your work culture may have made this bully into a bully, with a hyper-focus on performance and a blind eye to their bad behaviors. If this is the case, then working somewhere else in your organization might be exchanging one problem for a new one. You can do this by having conversations with other employees in other departments or simply making your own observations of other managers in your organization. I'll cover more of this topic, as it will play a significant factor in determining whether you stay with or leave your current company or organization.

Cope.

If you intend to stay and persevere in your situation, then you're going to need coping mechanisms. There are so many ways to cope within your given situation that I've created an entire chapter and the acronym EMPOWER to highlight all of the coping mechanisms that can help you. For me, each one of the coping elements that make up the acronym EMPOWER has helped me in my given bullying and harassment situations. Each of these elements can calm the mind in stressful situations, add perspective to your situation, and make you more resilient to bullying or harassment in the future. These elements have also helped me to see other opportunities outside my work situation.

Talk.

Talking to friends and family can also help you to cope. It's important to surround yourself with positivity to counter the negativity of your work situation. Trusted friends and family can be a sounding board as well as support. Going back to chapter 1 regarding the prevalence of this issue, it's quite likely that some of your closest friends and family members have been through these issues before. I know this was the case for me—many of my trusted colleagues, friends, and family had been through bullying or harassment in their past and present and were therefore able to empathize and help me in my bullying and harassment situations. And talking to a trusted colleague, friend, or family member can help you in the following ways as they had helped me:

- **Vent**. Taking the time to gather your thoughts and relay them to a family member, friend, or confidant can alone be cathartic. There is power in "speaking your truth": verbalizing what has been going on can help you help yourself more than leaving it within the thought realm. Speaking aloud the facts and your emotions on the matter can have a different effect on the way you process the situation than just thinking about the issue. It's for this reason that skilled therapists will allow their clients to do most of the speaking, because they realize the impact that "speaking your truth" has on your personal resolution to the issue.

- **Emotional support**. Friends and trusted colleagues can offer empathy and sympathy in the given situation. They can offer a safe space for you to share your thoughts and feelings without judgment. Family and friends' "listening ears" and emotional support can help to lower your emotions and associated stress in a charged situation.

- **Get perspective**. Sharing the specifics of a situation can help you get another viewpoint that's not your own. Getting outside of yourself and getting another person's opinion on the matter can help you determine whether it's general workplace conflict or whether it's crossed over into harassment or bullying. To get an even better perspective, it would help if this friend is a work confidant who is familiar with the person doing the bullying or harassment.

- **Get validation of your feelings**. In some cases of workplace bullying, the victims of the bullying may doubt their own perceptions. Talking to someone else can help you validate that what you're thinking and feeling is real.

- **Talking to another individual can help you to evaluate the overall culture of your workplace**. If it's a friend or family member outside your company, then you can compare your work environment and experiences with theirs. If it's a colleague within your organization, then you can compare your situation with their experiences within the organization, seeing if it's similar.

- **Get advice on the next steps in your specific situation**. I lay out general directions on a path to follow to resolve differences in the workplace, but a trusted friend or colleague can give you more specific steps tailored to your specific situation.

- **Strengthening relationships**. Talking to a colleague or friend about such situations can help strengthen a friendship with that individual. If it's a trusted individual at work, it can make the workplace more bearable.

- **Openness and transparency encourage others to be open and transparent**. Such openness can be an unveiling of what others have experienced in the organization. If the culture of your workplace is to "sweep issues under the carpet" or "don't rock the boat", then talking about your experiences can start a dialogue that encourages others who have felt victimized by bullying to come forward.

To the last point, the Me Too movement was born out of one person coming forward. Tarana Burke started the Me Too movement in 2006, and later it went viral through the hashtag #MeToo over ten years later in 2017. Coming forward at your workplace could similarly be a catalyst to your work culture.

Note that if you talk to someone at work, make sure that they're a trusted individual, keeping what you say in confidence.

- **Who to talk to and when at work**. When it comes to work, your employer has likely set up a process for raising bullying or harassment concerns that you should follow. It usually starts with trying to address the issue with the bully or harasser themselves. If the bully/harasser doesn't modify their behavior, then go to your immediate supervisor. After talking to your supervisor, the next person to talk to would be your HR representative. If your immediate supervisor is your bully, then you would be talking to your immediate supervisor to try to resolve it prior to going to your HR representative.

- **Talking to the bully or harasser**. When talking to a bully or harasser, be direct in letting them know what behavior bothers you and ask them to stop. If you are uncomfortable with conflict, you'll probably need to practice. Be respectful and direct, telling them what things they say or do bother you and let them know how their behavior makes you feel. I'll talk more about how to use your body language to show self-confidence and advocate for yourself in chapter 7.

- **Talking to your supervisor**. If your harasser or bully doesn't modify their behavior after talking to them, then turn to your immediate supervisor. Give your immediate supervisor a chance to resolve it or ask for their opinion in the matter. Tell them what's been going on and ask for their advice and/or help before going to your HR representative. They may feel frustrated or left out if you were to go to HR before talking to them. If you've kept a record of the harassment or bullying, then let your boss know that and summarize what you've documented. The facts of what has happened, when and how they've made you feel will be a helpful record to reference.

- **Talk to HR**. If your harasser or bully hasn't modified their behavior and you've talked to your immediate supervisor and gotten the green light from them to talk to HR, then go talk to HR. Your Human Resources representative can be another individual you can turn to regarding any issues at work. Not every HR person is a people person. Some have the personality of a "director" and they want you to be brief, be succinct, and be gone. Others have more people-person skills and want to hear your concerns and will even set up meetings for you to vent and share your concerns and feelings much like a trusted colleague or friend. You'll have to discern your HR representative's personality and adjust what you say to their personality and your work culture.

Things to consider before going to your Human Resource representative:

- What is my workplace culture? Is my workplace transparent, sharing cases of the past that have been resolved? Is my workplace supportive of individuals who have experienced harassment or bullying? Or are bullying and harassment part of the culture and accepted as commonplace?
- Familiarize yourself with your company's harassment and bullying policies. From reviewing these, you should know:
  - what your company's definitions are for bullying and harassment
  - whether your situation fits one of those definitions
  - the process for elevating bullying or harassment concerns
  - whether or not you're following your company's policies for elevating concerns

When facing workplace bullying or harassment, the following are benefits to talking to a Human Resources representative as opposed to talking to a colleague or friend. From your HR representative you can get:

1. **Professional expertise**. HR representatives are trained to help in workplace conflict, bullying, and harassment.
2. **Objectivity and neutrality**. They are expected to be a neutral party for work conflict, not taking any one person's side, and offering an objective assessment of the situation.
3. **Confidentiality and privacy**. Professionally, they are supposed to keep anything you say confidential and private.
4. **Interpretation of company policies and procedures**. They will know how the company policies and procedures apply within the context of your specific situation.
5. **Professional help and direction**. They'll let you know what your next steps are for resolution, and they'll work with you to resolve your situation at the earliest point possible in the RECTIFY process.
6. **Mediation and resolution facilitation**. In some cases, HR representatives can act as mediators to facilitate communication and resolution between you and other parties involved in bullying or harassment situations. They can help initiate conversations, conduct investigations, and explore options for conflict resolution, such as coaching, counseling, training or disciplinary actions. Their

involvement can lead to a fair and structured process to address the issue effectively.

7. **Documentation and legal protection**. Seeking assistance from an HR representative ensures that your concerns are officially documented. This documentation can be crucial in establishing a record of bullying or harassment, which may be necessary if the situation escalates or legal action is pursued. HR representatives can guide you on how to maintain documentation and navigate potential legal implications.

Your HR representative's support will depend on company culture, policies, and specific circumstances. It's important to note that one of your HR representative's key objectives is to represent and protect your company, keeping them compliant with employee laws and regulations. And general workplace bullying is not illegal (except in a few specific situations as Dr. Lynne Curry points out in her book, *Beating The Workplace Bully*). So your HR representative's advice could be affected by their goal to protect the company. And because a supervisor is seen as an agent for the company, HR will more likely take the side of a supervisor in a given supervisor-employee dispute.

Intermediary.

Work with your Human Resources representative and/or your manager to identify an intermediary if the issue can't be resolved directly with the person doing the harassment or bullying. When looking for an intermediary, you should find someone who is impartial, neutral, and is given authority over the situation. If possible, the intermediary should have some experience in mediating disputes or conflict. Both the target of the bullying/harassment and the person accused of the bullying/harassment present their case to the mediator. In the end, the mediator can recommend a path forward that could include disciplinary action, restitution, or training.

File.

File an official complaint if your situation can't be resolved by the intermediary. Work with your HR representative to find and fill in forms necessary for formally filing a complaint.

beYond.

Sometime beyond your filing of an official complaint, you should circle back to see whether appropriate actions have been taken. A month is about the right duration to check back in and monthly cadence thereafter until the issue is closed.

Recap

Again, it's not necessary to go through every element of the RECTIFY process. It's possible and beneficial to both you, the person with whom you have the conflict, and the organization to rectify your disagreement at the earliest point possible. Regarding the order of the actions that make up the word RECTIFY, the REC will likely be ongoing and done in parallel with all the elements of RECTIFY, whereas the TIFY should be done in consecutive order. For instance, if bullying or harassment persists, then you want to record those new incidences. Likewise, the E of evaluation is something that you'll want to do periodically, to put some numbers to any improvement or worsening of your situation. If the bullying or harassment is ongoing, you can self-evaluate how the latest episode has affected you. You can also self-evaluate how any of the new coping activities improve your personal outlook on your situation. And regarding coping activities, you will want to continue these throughout the process to see how they're helping to improve your situation.

Chapter 3 Homework

1. Document the details of a bullying or harassment situation that you've experienced or observed as follows:

   a. What happened?

    b.   When? (dates and times)

    c.   Who said what to whom?

    d.   How did it make you feel?

    e.   What of the chapter 1 twelve mental and twelve physical negative effects of bullying did you experience?

2. Write out the elements that make up the acronym RECTIFY.

3. For any situations of the past or present where you experienced or observed bullying or harassment, name the elements of the RECTIFY process that were used toward resolving the situation.

CHAPTER 4

SHOULD I STAY OR SHOULD I GO?

Who are you?

If you answered that question with something you do, whether you answered with what you do for a living or what or who you are in your personal life—a mother, father, daughter, son, etc.—then go deeper yet. At your very core, you're a "being". "You are". Or from your point of view, "I am". So it is at the miracle of this self-awareness that I'll start this chapter. Indeed, at your very core, you're more than even your own body. At your core, you're a being, not a "doing". You need to separate yourself from being known by what you do and simply marvel at the miracle of your "being" at your core. So in this chapter, I want you to disassociate yourself from the paradigm of thinking that you are what you do.

The life that you currently find yourself in was created by Y-O-U. You are the captain of your ship. You have relied on your own God-given qualities to arrive at the point where you now find yourself: your talents, your logic, your knowledge, your experiences, etc. What you do for a living at this moment is based on a career path that you navigated due to the intersection of multiple factors. But at the core of this is the ship's captain, you. To realize that is both empowering and emboldening.

The situation of bullying or harassment that you bought this book to help you through is not your fault. You didn't ask to have this individual come into your work life and spill their toxicity. Had you known this person was going to be there for your future "you", you may have done something to try to avert it. Like, possibly, take that previous job offer two years before. I bring up that you are the captain of your ship now to point out the obvious: you've captained your ship to this point and navigated other issues of your past work relationships to get here—and you'll do it again now— in this current situation.

In the previous chapter, I walked through the stepwise procedure to follow to rectify your situation within the context of continuing to work within your current position. In this chapter, I'll explore options outside of your current employer. In some ways you may have to break the paradigm of who you are and what you do to earn an income. But before I get to that, you need to decide for yourself if your current situation is too much for you and whether your situation can be rectified.

Key Things to Consider in Your Decision

Note: If you're using this book for a bullying or harassment situation outside of work, you can use this chapter in the context of your specific situation. For example, if it's a bullying situation at school, you can follow this chapter in the context of choosing other schooling alternatives. If you're experiencing bullying online, you can use this chapter to determine whether you should stay or go from the online platform where you're experiencing bullying or harassment.

Working at a company in a lot of ways is analogous to a marriage. Even when the same problems persist over time without resolution, there are a host of reasons why you decide to stay—in both a marriage and in a job. But just as you wouldn't want to stay in a loveless marriage, you wouldn't want to stay in an unfulfilling job. And even more so if bullying or harassment is the norm for your organization or company.

You may feel like you're locked in your job, but you're not. There are so many other things out there you could do. But there are some things to consider before looking at leaving your current company or organization. As in a marriage, you want to see if you can work out your differences. So working through the RECTIFY process is key. The key element of RECTIFY that will help determine whether you should stay is the E for evaluation. The degree to which you're being bullied or harassed should be one of the main determining factors as to whether you stay. So the bullying assessment should play a major role in your decision.

And even more important in your decision as to whether you stay or go should be your personal mental assessment—how has this bullying or harassment situation affected your mental well-being? Going back to chapter 1, that is one of the main reasons why bullying and harassment are so key—the adverse effects they have on both your personal mental and physical health. The larger the impact your situation is having on your mental health, the more effort you should put into finding other work alternatives. In addition to your self-evaluation, you should do some self-evaluation of other elements of your job, such as asking yourself:

1. How much do I like my job?
2. What are the favorite things about my job?
3. Do I like the rest of my organization minus the bully or harasser?
4. Does the culture of my organization encourage bullying? (This could be purposeful or inadvertent.)

5. Am I willing to move or commute?
6. Am I willing to take a pay cut?
7. My work reputation would have to be rebuilt at a new place.
8. What is my promotion potential in my current company?
9. Is my career path negatively affected by my bullying situation? If so, how?
10. The impact that bullying or harassment is having on my personal well-being. Do some self-reflection over and above the E in RECTIFY.

It would be good to write out the answers to these questions and add more that are specific to your situation. Then sort the answers into the positives and negatives of your job, essentially building a pros and cons list of staying. That way, on one sheet you have all your thoughts regarding staying or going. A pros and cons list can be a great analytical tool for any major life decision such as: getting married vs. staying single, buying a new house, or something fun like one vacation vs. another. This pros and cons list can be a living document too—whenever new information becomes available, you can add or update it. You could also look at more than two options, such as: 1) stay in the current position, 2) stay with the company but work in a different department, or 3) leaving the company for a totally new position.

You can use your answer to these questions as headers on your pros and cons list for staying or leaving.

As I said in an earlier story, I fantasized daily about leaving my job. I loved what I did, I loved the people in the organization, loved the community it was in and my pay and benefits fit my responsibilities. But the weekly and sometimes daily interactions with my boss had me thinking about leaving the company every time I had a negative interaction.

Self-Evaluating Your Work Culture

When considering leaving or staying with your current company, you should do a deeper evaluation of your organization's or company's work culture. A clear understanding of your work culture can help you to determine the prevalence of your situation. Sometimes there's a stark difference from one organization to the next within a company. That was the case for me in automotive. In the New Product Development environment, I never experienced or witnessed overt bullying or harassment. Whereas in my limited experience in the plants, overt bullying and harassment were the norm. And friends who had worked in both environments told me that they had experienced the same thing. Here are some things to consider when doing a deeper dive into better understanding your workplace culture toward your stay-or-go decision:

1. **Observe your fellow coworkers and managers**. Take note of the way people interact with one another. Note their tone more than their topics. Are they supportive and respectful or do you see bullying, micromanaging, and gossiping? Is your bullying or harassment circumstance the norm or is it the exception? Is your bullying or harassment situation being handled in a fair and judicious way or is the issue being swept under the carpet? Look for both positive and negative interactions. Are positive interactions the norm? If you're aware of someone else having a bullying or harassment situation, ask whether or not it was resolved and, if so, what was done to resolve it.

2. **Ask other colleagues**. What has been their experience with managers? If you've only been there for a few years, ask someone who's been there longer and ask them if they've seen a trend over time. What do they like about the work environment or culture? What do they find challenging? Are there any specific things they think should be addressed?

3. **Attending company events, meetings, or outings**. Do these events promote a positive, inclusive atmosphere or do they say things that would stereotype or exclude certain individuals?

4. **Policy vs. Practice**. Check the company's policies. Do they talk a good talk? In other words, are the policies transparent, consistent, and fair? Does what you observe align with what you read in the policies? Is what is written in the policies disconnected from reality, or are the policies simply a façade misrepresenting what's going on?

5. **Promotions and awards**. Are people with positive "work together" traits getting promoted? Are persons promoted only for results in spite of known and observable negative traits (as in my lead-off story)? Does everyone seem to get a "fair shake" when it comes time for promotions?

6. **Workplace conflict**. Is there clear guidance for workplace conflict regarding how to handle it when it arises? If so, do conflict resolution techniques have a spirit of "working together"? Do the company's policies distinguish between normal conflict vs. bullying and harassment? Is there training for handling workplace conflict? Is there training for bullying and harassment, specifically for managers? For all employees?

7. **Look at employee turnover rates**. Do they seem abnormally high? High turnover rates could indicate a toxic environment.

8. **Are there other organizations within my company** with a better reputation for handling workplace conflict, bullying, or harassment? If so, what job opportunities and career paths are available in those situations?

Other Options to Leaving

Leaving one job for another job, by the way, isn't your only option. Sometimes with a new job, you leave one bad situation only to get into another different bad situation—possibly worse. It's difficult to ascertain what the culture of a new place is unless you were to work there. Besides getting a new job, you should consider other sources of income that could help you rise above the need to be dependent on a job. You really should consider additional options that you may have not been thinking of:

1. **Take a sabbatical**. Take some time off from work. This can help you have both the time and headspace to see past situations more clearly.
2. **Put more into retirement**. Tighten your belt and put more money into your 401K, bringing your retirement closer.
3. **Start a side business or side hustle**. By starting something on the side, you can find other areas of interest.

4. **Look to future consulting in your area of expertise**. Reach out through others who are already contracting toward getting your name out there. Networking will be your key to future contracts. The more you network, the more opportunities you'll have.

5. **Real estate**. Selling real estate on the side or flipping or renting your house and downsizing.

6. **Passive income**. A laundromat or vending machine business are examples of this.

7. **"Gig" economy income**. Pet sitting, renting a room in your house, delivering food or driving people via Lyft or Uber are examples of jobs that can get you Gig money.

8. **Teaching or tutoring**.

9. **Starting a service company**. Pool cleaning, junk removal, lawn mowing, deck cleaning, etc. are all examples of this. Services are always in high demand.

10. **Writing a book in your field of expertise**. A book in your area of expertise can improve your current job situation and respect that you get from your peers and management AND it can make you more marketable to outside companies. A book works better than a business card and resume at finding you your next job, or it can work toward helping you start a contracting business.

11. **Write a book on something in your life that you've overcome**. That's basically what I'm doing with this book. Do what I've done. Writing a book can be fulfilling, monetizing, and get your name out there more so than not writing a book. I honestly think there's more than one book in each of us. If writing a book isn't on your bucket list, it should be. I mean, here I am writing a book when writing and English were my weakest subjects throughout school, including high school and college, where I went into engineering as opposed to becoming a lawyer like my father because of my weakness in writing.

12. **If you're over fifty-five years old**, start your pension or 401K without penalty and start doing something else in a semi-retired state.

Recap

Whatever route you choose, you should do some amount of research and even trial out some of the above options while you're still working at your current company. That way you always have your current income to fall back on for anything that you don't end up liking or doesn't pay off.

By earning money in another form, you are relieving the stress of your current situation as you can see monetization of other alternatives to your current job. The amount of additional work you put into other income sources should match your current level of work dissatisfaction. By looking into these additional sources of income and pursuing them, you're able to get a better perspective of your situation and see your situation for what it is—a blip in your life of experiences.

Remember that at your core you are not a "doing" but a "being"—it's okay and even freeing to break the current paradigm of being known by your current work.

Chapter 4 Homework

1. Evaluate your current work situation using the ten questions cited in earlier in this chapter and copied here for your convenience:

   a. How much do I like my job?

   b. What are the favorite things about my job?

   c. Do I like the rest of my organization minus the bully or harasser?

   d. Does the culture of my organization encourage bullying? (This could be purposeful or inadvertent.)

   e. Am I willing to move or commute?

f. Am I willing to take a pay cut?

g. My work reputation would have to be rebuilt at a new place.

h. What is my promotion potential in my current company?

i. Is my career path negatively affected by my bullying situation? If so, how?

j. The impact that bullying or harassment is having on my personal well-being. Do some self-reflection over and above the E in RECTIFY.

2. Evaluate your current workplace culture:

a. Observe your fellow coworkers and managers. Look specifically at how they resolve conflict. Do they do so in a healthy, respectful manner?

b. Ask a colleague. What has been their experience with managers and conflict resolution?

c. For any company events you've attended, do you hear encouragement for all people groups?

d. Check the company's policies. Do they talk a good talk? Are the policies followed?

e. Promotions and awards. Are people with positive "work together" traits getting promoted?

f. Is there clear guidance for workplace conflict regarding how to handle it when it arises? If so, do conflict resolution techniques have a spirit of working together? Do the company's policies distinguish between normal conflict vs. bullying and harassment?

g. Look at employee turnover rates. Do they seem abnormally high? As far as you know, did anyone leave the company because of the work culture?

h. Are there other organizations within my company with a better reputation for handling workplace conflict, bullying, or harassment?

3. Name two additional sources of income from the list given in the chapter that sound appealing to you.

CHAPTER 5

CONFLICT RESOLUTION

In this chapter I'll address general work conflict which refers to non-harassment and non-bullying type conflict. This chapter pulled out by itself could not only help you navigate work conflict but any form of conflict that you find in your life (for example, with a spouse, landlord, friend, parent, sibling, neighbor). This chapter is more applicable for the cases of general workplace conflict but can also be helpful in the cases where you need to confront a bully or harasser. In the end, the advice of this chapter will help you find solutions that will benefit both parties in a given conflict (i.e., a win-win solution).

Understanding Conflict.

Conflict refers to disagreement or clash between two or more parties with opposing interests, goals, needs or perspectives. Conflict in the workplace is due to one or more factors such as, but not limited to, the following: interpersonal differences, organizational changes, power struggles, miscommunication, hidden agendas, jealousy, opposing priorities, work frustration, home frustrations, personality differences, limited resources, differing work styles, unresolved grievances, etc. With these many factors, it's a wonder that we don't have more conflict at work.

Adding another layer to these factors is what your work environment is. If you work in a supportive work environment, then the above factors will likely be muted. If you work in a toxic work environment, then the above factors will likely be worse. The root cause of the type of environment you find yourself in is leadership. Strong, respectful leadership can be found in the supportive workplace, and negative or weak leadership, which includes jealousy, blaming, anger, etc., can be found at the top of a toxic work environment.

Constructive vs. Destructive Conflict

In constructive conflict, both parties will focus on the issue at hand and not the persons on the opposing sides. The hallmark of constructive conflict is peaceful communication including not only what is said, but the volume, tone, and body language on both sides. Destructive conflict, on the other hand, will include negative behaviors on one or more sides in a given conflict. You will know whether your conflict is constructive or destructive when you feel it and see it.

In both cases, there exist opposing views on a given matter; however, with constructive conflict, opposing parties will feel less tension than they will in destructive conflict. Healthy, constructive conflict can lead to growth, innovation, and improved relationships. On the other hand, unhealthy, destructive conflict, such as workplace bullying and harassment, erodes trust, damages relationships, and undermines the overall well-being of those involved and the organization. It's for this reason that this section by itself would be helpful for a company or organization to use as guidance for all their employees to use when dealing with workplace conflict.

Unresolved conflict

Unresolved conflict at work (just as unresolved conflict with a spouse) will fester over time. It's both in the company's, the organization's, and the individual's best interest to keep "short accounts", meaning to resolve differences often, quickly, and in a balanced way. Resentment can build in those who are giving more than they're taking in any situation or relationship. Going back to the story that I led this book off with, the leader in the program office habitually yelled, humiliated, and belittled those with opposing opinions to his own. In fact, it seemed that he did this so often, it became a habit. I remember overhearing one such meeting where he began the meeting by yelling and belittling those who had entered his office—even before they were given a chance to speak. I remember those in the meeting agreeing with his position simply to calm him down. This director was using the conflict resolution technique called "bulldozing" that I'll elaborate more on in the next section of this chapter. Similar to an overbearing spouse, this director was unknowingly feeding resentment and anger in those on the receiving end of his bulldozing. Unresolved conflict can lead to decreased productivity, morale, or worse, crossing over into more extreme behaviors as in the case of my older coworker who shot two managers before taking his own life.

The corollary also holds that a work environment with good conflict resolution skills will be a productive, innovative, and creative work environment. Note the feedback loop between work conflicts and work environment. Unresolved conflict feeds negative work environment which feeds the negative factors influencing conflict. On the other hand, the positive feedback loop exists between resolved conflict to positive work environment to the factors influencing conflict.

Conflict Resolution Techniques

There are multiple options to follow when addressing conflict at and outside of work. What is your go-to method of dealing with conflict? The ones listed in this section are some popular ones.

1. **Conflict avoidance**. In this method, you procrastinate dealing with conflict in the hope that it will go away. And at times, it will. This may be a good approach for less important issues. In other words, you don't want to take a stand on every opinion that you have, or you could come across as argumentative, opinionated, a know-it-all, or rigid. For issues that are important to you personally or professionally including bullying or harassment, conflict avoidance only kicks the can down the street, becoming tomorrow's problem. Or the other person takes the lead on the issue and their direction is what is followed. Not addressing issues that are important to you can build resentment in yourself toward the other person without them even knowing it. If you find yourself in a bullying or harassment situation, conflict avoidance will not only delay resolution to the issue, but it will possibly embolden or empower the harasser or bully.

2. **Conflict accommodation, consent or acquiescence**. To agree with the opposing view verbally (consent) or by your silence by not disagreeing (acquiesce), you are misrepresenting your position. This is very similar to conflict avoidance in that you're not letting your position be known. The nuance difference between these two approaches is that in consent or acquiescence, the opposing view is being stated to you and you agree verbally or by your silence. Whereas in conflict avoidance, you're actually trying to steer clear of the potential conflict—never bringing it up. The motivation for both conflict resolution techniques might be the same: avoiding the stress of conflict. But both methods only delay a resolution or give in to the other side's approach.

   If you're an introvert by nature, then it may require courage and strength to stand up and let your voice be known. If either of these approaches are your go-to approaches for conflict resolution, you would be a great candidate for the assertiveness training recommended in the training chapter of this book. Another factor in conflict avoidance, consent, and acquiescence is who is on the other side of the argument; for instance, is it someone above you in the organization or is the person known for being a "bulldozer", as I mentioned earlier?

3. **Compromise**. In this method of conflict resolution, you try to meet the other side halfway or somewhere in between their position and yours. In this situation, you're verbalizing your position to the other side. This may or may not be the best for both parties. If, for instance, you're the landlord and the person leasing your apartment is late in paying their rent, taking half the rent now is not the best for you, as it sets a precedence for the future that you're willing to take half of the rent.

4. **Bulldozing**. If your typical method of conflict resolution is to try to force the other side to your way of thinking, then you're what I would call a bulldozer. If this is your typical method for conflict resolution, then you're likely to leave a trail of resentment. This can easily become bullying or harassment if it's done with a raised voice, threats, belittling, or humiliation.

5. **Convincer**. Winning the other side over to your way of thinking through your data or logical argument employs the "convincer" form of conflict resolution. This approach has its place if, for instance, your audience doesn't have all of the data for a decision, and they aren't

leaning one direction more than another. This is my typical approach with my classes and when I would have a presentation to management.

6. **Winner takes all**. This could be done as quickly as "rock, paper, scissors" or some other form of winner-gets-to-choose game. This is a good one for fun decisions like the paint color of a room or what show or movie to watch next or at work for deciding who covers what topic in a presentation, but it shouldn't be used for more serious decisions.

There's nothing inherently wrong with any of these approaches, and they each have their place and time. Even bulldozing has its place—if it's done calmly peacefully and you happen to be the boss (or parent) and the task needs to be done. But there is a better approach that will help both sides arrive at a win-win solution.

Collaboration and problem-solving technique. The same skills that you use at work to solve problems and innovate can be used to settle conflict at work. In this conflict resolution technique, both sides work together towards coming up with solutions that would benefit both sides – with the goal of coming up with that idea that would benefit both sides for a given conflict.

Brainstorming can be a tool to help opposing sides work collaboratively toward generating ideas from which they can later choose an idea or multiple ideas that benefit both sides. And to come up with the best ideas possible, you should employ the following rules of brainstorming for general workplace conflict (i.e., conflict that hasn't escalated into bullying or harassment):

1. **Problem statement**. In one sentence, state the problem in the form of a question. In the story at the beginning of book, the argument that had led to the bullying and shooting was centered around an engineering issue. Those on one side of the engineering issue wanted to use a certain type of components because they were significantly cheaper; those on the other side didn't want to use the cheaper components because they were historically less reliable than other components. So when I later led a tiger team to decide whether or not the Navy should use these cheaper components, I used the following initial problem statements to help us determine the best course of action as a team: 1) What are the benefits of using these cheaper components? 2) What are the risks of using these cheaper components?

2. **Focus on the problem statement and not each other**. When brainstorming, it's important to

keep the focus on coming up with ideas and avoiding making negative remarks.

3. **The brainstorming team**. The brainstorming team should consist of experts on both sides of a given argument, as well as individuals who are not experts and unformed opinions on the given topic. This was the case with this tiger team—I included two experts, one who supported the use of the cheaper components and another who was against the use of these cheaper components. Also, I included individuals who were not experts and had not yet formed opinions on the use of the cheaper components.

4. **No bad ideas**. During the brainstorming session, there are no bad ideas. In fact, during the brainstorming session crazy ideas are encouraged as they can lead to team members thinking of ideas that wouldn't have been thought of otherwise. If team members start evaluating ideas during the brainstorming session, remind them that the brainstorming session is only for ideas and that ideas will be evaluated after the brainstorming session.

5. **Encourage participation from all parties**. There will typically be both vocal and less vocal members in teams. To get participation from less vocal members, you can employ round-

table brainstorming, where you go around the room giving each person on the team a chance to share an idea.

6. **Keep ideas short and succinct**, between two and four words if possible so that the facilitator can capture the idea quickly. Team members should avoid long explanations or elaborations during the brainstorming. This will allow for more time for more ideas. Ideas can be explained or elaborated on after the brainstorming session is over.

7. **Generate many ideas**. The key here is to generate as many ideas as possible in the given brainstorming session.

8. **Encourage "piggybacking"**. Piggybacking is building off the ideas of others.

9. **Check your titles at the door**. To maximize the impact of a given brainstorming session, each person in the room should be seen as an equal. It may be necessary to say this at the beginning of a brainstorming session.

10. **Brainstorming should be done with a facilitator** for a set amount of time and all ideas written where all participants can see. If the brainstorming is done in an online format, one person who is capturing the ideas should do so on the screen they're sharing. The time for the brainstorming session should be between five

and ten minutes. Some teams may decide to include a timekeeper on the team who will let the team know when the time is up. Others may use an approximate time and end the brainstorming when the rate of new ideas slows down or stops.

Before the brainstorming session starts, have both sides of a given matter share the facts. The idea is to get all of the team members at the same level of knowledge on the issue. Additionally, the team members should agree on what rules of brainstorming they'll use. A team could follow some, all, or none of these ten rules I've listed above and/or add their own rules.

Following these rules of brainstorming, participants can effectively collaborate on solutions, generating a wide range of ideas to choose from. After the brainstorming session is over, you can use a voting or rating process to land on ideas that would be seen as a win from both sides of a given conflict. In a voting system, you can give each team member three votes after the brainstorming session. You want each person to write down their voted-on ideas before people start sharing to avoid "group think" where voted-on ideas are influenced by other team members' votes. The ideas with the most votes will reflect what's important for the team on the given topic. In the end, you want to land on ideas that represent shared interests and foster win-win outcomes for both sides of the conflict.

Even with the most potentially volatile topics, consensus can be reached. In the tiger team that I led, we were able to come to consensus on an approach regarding the use of the cheaper components that we could all agree on. Again, brainstorming should be used only for general workplace conflict, it shouldn't be used for bullying or harassment. If the conflict has escalated into bullying or harassment, then the person being bullied or harassed should meet separately with the bully or harasser and specifically address the bullying or harassment that occurred, following the process outlined in the T of RECTIFY. A mediator may be necessary in case the issue can't be resolved between the bully/harasser and bullied/harassed.

Mediation and facilitation. An independent mediator could also be used to resolve general workplace conflict as well. In such a situation, the mediator will guide the parties toward a mutually acceptable position.

Decision authority. In this, both sides present their case to a leader in the organization and the leader makes the decision, citing the rationale for their decision.

Skills for Better Conflict Resolution - PEACE

There are key skills you can learn and develop that will help you improve your conflict resolution techniques. Again, I use an acronym to help you to remember these skills. In this case, the acronym is PEACE, and it stands for:

> Proactive
> Emotional intelligence
> Attitude
> Communication skills
> Exploration of solutions skills

Proactive

Be proactive in addressing significant conflict whether:

- at home with a spouse, roommate, neighbor, or relative
- at work with a colleague, boss, fellow team member, leader, or subordinate
- at school with a fellow student or teacher
- in any other social venue with a friend, acquaintance, or otherwise

The conflict could be general disagreement, an issue you have with someone else (such as in bullying or harassment), or an issue someone else has with you. I added the word "significant" above knowing that addressing each conflict is going to require a certain amount of energy and addressing every conflict would be unreasonable. You'll have to personally decide what conflicts are "significant". In the end, though, you don't want to shy away from conflict that impacts your personal physical or mental health, finances, job performance, or career path. If you addressed every conflict in your life, you wouldn't have much time or energy for anything else. Some conflicts just aren't worth the time or effort. Things to consider when deciding whether the conflict is worth addressing:

1. is it with a person that you will have to see frequently
2. how close you are to the person with whom you have a disagreement
3. the significance of the disagreement, harassment, or bullying—is it worth your energy
4. the likelihood that it will happen again if not addressed

In the end, you decide what's worth the effort.

Also, part of being proactive is choosing the time and place. You want to choose a time of day and place that is convenient for you and those on the other side of the conflict. If it's a disagreement at home, you want to choose a time when both sides are awake and at their best—avoiding discussions immediately after someone comes home from work, late at night, or before a planned fun activity. Another factor in being proactive is preparing yourself—reviewing, practicing, and preparing yourself to apply the EACE of PEACE.

Emotional Intelligence

Emotional intelligence is the ability to recognize, understand, and deal skillfully with one's own emotions and the emotions of others (as by regulating one's own emotions or by showing empathy or good judgment in social interactions). (Merriam-Webster)

There are two major facets to our emotional intelligence that will contribute to our success in working through conflict:

- Our personal ability to understand and regulate our own emotions
- Our ability to empathize with the emotions of others

Both require us to "get outside of ourselves". On the surface, it sounds easy, but when you're in the heat of the moment while in a conflict, it can be very challenging and difficult to practice. And just like with Intelligence Quotient (IQ), each of us has varying degrees of Emotional Intelligence (EI). The more you're able to get outside of yourself and see the situation from an external perspective, the higher your Emotional Intelligence. It's possible to raise your

Emotional Intelligence, thus improving your ability to resolve conflict successfully both in life and at work. To raise your Emotional Intelligence, you will have to:

- understand emotions and their impact on conflict resolution
- improve your emotional regulation
- improve your empathy and perspective-taking

Understanding Emotions

By understanding the role that emotions will play in conflicts, you can better evaluate the conflict from a strictly logical point of view. Toward this understanding, it's helpful to know that we typically operate on one side of the brain at a time when problem-solving. Each individual is dominant on one hemisphere of their brain, either being right-brained or left-brained: our left brain is the more logical side and our right brain is the more creative, emotive side. Additionally, the left side of the brain has a propensity to focus on positive emotions whereas the right side of the brain focuses more on negative emotions.

When it comes to a disagreement, it is important to operate more on the left side using logic and positive emotions and steer away from the emotive, more negative right brain. If you're a right-brained person, this may be a challenge because you're dominant in your creative, emotional side. For a left-brain dominant person, this may be a natural inclination to think with the logical side. The character Spock from *Star Trek* was almost entirely left-brained, seeing each situation from only the logical point of view. He looked at decisions as the summation of a long equation of factors that excluded factors relating to the emotions of himself or others.

Emotional regulation

The one thing that pure left-brain thinking like Spock's can help you with is the ability to regulate your own emotions—keeping the emotions from any conflict or argument. Going back to the *Star Trek* example, how many times did we see Captain Kirk get red-in-the face angry during the life-and-death situations that his crew faced, and how many times did we likewise see Spock let full vent to his emotions in such situations.

- Captain Kirk – at least once every episode
- Spock – never

In some workplaces, individuals are facing life-or-death situations daily (e.g., doctors, nurses, emergency workers)—it's even more important to be like Spock in the daily decision-making of these career fields. Disagreements will occur at work but "emotional regulation", the controlling of one's own emotions, is key to keeping our own emotions out of a work disagreement.

Empathy and perspective-taking

Another side of Emotional Intelligence requires the right side of the brain—your ability to have genuine empathy for the other person in a given conflict. In the case of harassment or bullying, this will be more challenging. And in some cases where the bullying or harassment is extreme and the bully or harasser is unrepentant, this is a nearly impossible task. Just as I personified emotional regulation with the character Spock, I'll personify empathy—genuine empathy—with Leo Buscaglia (Baines, Ph. D. and McBrayer, Ph. D.). If you haven't heard one of Leo's talks, look him up on YouTube. Leo was a professor at USC in the 1960s-'80s. Following the suicide death of a student, he thought of how disconnected we humans are and, in response, started the non-credit course called Love 1A.

I saw one of Leo's videos in elementary school and it had such a profound impact on me that I remember it to this day. In this video, his message was the importance of demonstrating love in actions and the importance of doing so even with strangers. To illustrate this point, he told a story of a cross-country flight he had on Christmas day. After talking to the stewardess, he realized how sad she was to be working on Christmas day and how sad she was to not be spending the day with family. So he thought about what he could do to lift her spirits. He decided to decorate the cabin with holiday items he had in his luggage while she was in the back getting the food cart ready. When she saw the effort that Leo, a stranger to her, had put into spreading some Christmas cheer, she cried. And so it is with you in your situation to "love" the other person—to put yourself into their shoes on the given disagreement. And not only put yourself into their shoes but to walk a mile in them.

Of course, this is all a mental exercise, but seeing the other side of an argument or disagreement is essential for resolution. Harness your inner Leo Buscaglia to give genuine empathy on your given conflict. Empathy for the other side of a disagreement will require a hybrid of both left- and right-brained thinking. It will require your right brain for you to imagine yourself in the shoes of the other side of the disagreement, and it will require the left side of your brain to have positive emotions regarding that individual. If you have trouble doing this, recall from chapter 1 that the person on the other side of the disagreement is, like you, a protagonist in their own story. No one sees themselves as an antagonist.

Again, it's possible for you to raise your Emotional Intelligence. It starts with the awareness of these factors which you now have since you've read this section, and it requires practice.

Attitude

When working through conflict, take a step back and examine your attitude toward the other person and your attitude toward the conflict. Try to separate the person from the conflict. Do your best at having a positive attitude for a given situation, as any negativity will come through your body language, posture, facial expression, or things you say.

Communication Skills

Effective communication is crucial in addressing workplace conflicts and resolving issues related to bullying and harassment. And believe it or not, the best communication skills when encountering conflict is NOT your ability to convince the other side to see your side of the conflict. There are four key communication skills that will help you have a successful resolution to conflict.

Communication Skill 1 – Active Listening. They say that 90 percent of communication is non-verbal. Meaning that your actions, your gestures, and the tone of your voice speak louder than the words you speak. So when you practice the communication skills of active listening, you are showing the other person that they are heard. The following are the Do's and Don'ts of active listening:

Do's:

- Listen with your eyes, posture, and facial expression.

- Listen attentively and actively. Avoid thinking through the points you're going to make when the person finishes and instead put your focus on what the other person is saying, keeping silent as they share. Speak only after the person has stopped talking and leaves a long pause, implying that they're finished talking.

- Try to stay relaxed, as any tension will show up in your facial expression, posture, or otherwise. The idea here is to create a safe space to resolve your differences.

- Repeat back in your own words what you think the person said. Knowing in advance that you'll be repeating back what they've said will force you to listen to what they're saying. And there's typically a tension in the other person related to wondering whether you heard what they were saying and whether you understand their position enough to repeat it back in your own words. By repeating back what they've said, you remove this tension and make the other person feel more relaxed. Knowing and repeating back what their position is and why they have taken that position will also help you have empathy for them – thus helping you with this aspect of your emotional intelligence. Lastly, repeating back what they've said will help them identify and clarify anything that you potentially missed.

Don'ts:

- Don't show any impatience while waiting for them to finish what they're saying.
- Don't be distracted by other things in the room or outside the room. This includes your phone. Turn off the ringer and lay it face down if necessary.
- Don't be ready to pounce or be waiting for them to finish so that you can share your opinions.

Communication Skill 2 – Peaceful Communication. Keep anger and frustration out of your speech. Calmness is key. If emotions in you or the other person kick in, then you both will be operating in the right sides of your brains, letting your emotions run free. It's important to harness your inner Spock, sticking to the facts of the conflict. Be aware of any tension on your face, as it will show up as a forced smile or a frown. Practice talking about the topic in front of a mirror or while looking at yourself on your phone. Typically, the other person will reflect back what they see in your facial expression—if your face is relaxed, they'll be more likely to be relaxed. If your face is tense, they will reflect tension.

Communication Skill 3 – Constructive Feedback. If you are in a situation where you must give feedback to the person., do so with a positive attitude. Make sure that it's constructive and building up the other person.

Communication Skill 4 – Empathy. Express empathy in your words, your tone, and your actions. Show the other person that you understand where they're coming from. Again, restating their points in your own words will communicate to them that they've been heard.

By taking the high road with your communication, you're demonstrating your personal leadership skills, whether you're in a leadership position or not. And if you're not in a leadership position yet, you'll be on your way to one by showing calmness in a potentially charged situation. Know that to improve your communication skills, you need to practice each of these.

Exploring-solutions skills

The following are three skills that will help in your solution exploration: 1) creativity 2) willingness to find a win-win 3) negotiation.

Creativity.

The number and type of solutions will be limited by your creativity. The more creative you are, the more and better solutions you will come up with.

Willingness to Find a Win-Win.

In order to come up with solutions that benefit all parties in a given conflict, you must first have a willingness for the other side(s) to get a win from the conflict too. Ideas that you come up with in a brainstorming session aren't set in stone. So think of and verbalize potential solutions that will benefit not only yourself but the other side(s).

Negotiating Skills.

Entire books could be written and have been written on negotiation skills. Many of the skills I brought up earlier will help in negotiation: active listening, empathy, peaceful communication, and working collaboratively toward win-win solutions. Other skills that will be helpful in negotiation:

- **Understanding the other side** – Do your homework in advance of meetings to discuss the conflict. Research the other side's arguments to rightly understand their concerns. And possibly set up a pre-meeting with the other side with the main objective being to listen and take notes. The more clearly you understand the other side, the better you'll be at empathizing and understanding.
- **Finding common ground** – Look for and emphasize the common points between both sides.

- **Discernment** – You'll need discernment to determine whether there are underlying, unspoken issues or motivations at play.
- **Patience** – The conflict may not be resolved in one or even two meetings. Patience and calm will bring you closer to resolution than impatience and restlessness.
- **Assertiveness and confidence** – Make certain that you are assertive and confident when representing your own position and opinion but balance that with respect for the other party's opinions and position. Be direct and confident with your body language, your tone, and your words when representing your position.
- **Adaptability and learning** – Learn from each meeting regarding the conflict and adapt your position accordingly.
- **Flexibility and compromise** – Don't fall in love with your own ideas. Be willing to consider new ideas where both parties win. Be open to and encourage common-ground, mutually beneficial solutions.

Summary.

By equipping yourself with effective communication, negotiation, and conflict resolution skills, you will be better prepared to address workplace conflict and even bullying and harassment in a constructive and empathetic manner. These skills foster a healthier work environment, enhance relationships, and contribute to your personal and professional growth and the growth of your organization.

Chapter 5 Homework

1. What is your typical go-to method for conflict resolution?

2. What are some of the drawbacks of this conflict resolution method?

3. What lessons from the chapter could you incorporate to improve your conflict resolution techniques?

4. Name the elements that make up the acronym PEACE.

   P_____ -

   E_____ _____ -

   A_____ -

   C_____ _____ -

   E_____ _____ _____ -

5. Self-rate yourself on a scale of one to ten for each of these elements, with a one for "needs improvement" and ten for "I've mastered this element".

6. Based on your self-rating, what elements of PEACE do you need to work on the most to improve your conflict resolution skills?

7. Write out an action for each of the elements of PEACE you identified in #3 above and apply that action in a future conflict (for example, "staying quiet, relaxed, and attentive as others share" as an action for communication).

8. Apply the actions from #3 and #7 above to future conflict at work or at home.

Extra Credit

Watch a Leo Buscaglia video of your choosing. Ten points.

SECTION 3

OVERCOME

"THE GREATER THE OBSTACLE,
THE MORE GLORY IN OVERCOMING IT"

~MOLIERE

CHAPTER 6

EMPOWER - POWER TOOLS FOR RISING ABOVE YOUR SITUATION

In this chapter, I'll introduce "Power Tools" to help you rise above your situation. These same power tools can be used to help you with any negative situation you find yourself in. I've categorized these power tools into the acronym EMPOWER to make it easier for you to remember each of these power tools. Empower stands for:

E – Exercise

M – Meditation

P – Positivity

O – Out

W – Welfare

E – Exhale

R – Reverse

In this chapter, I'll explain what each of these word categories means and how each will help you in your situation. I introduced the importance of coping mechanisms in chapter 3 as the C in RECTIFY. Here I'll introduce the elements of EMPOWER and elaborate on how they can help you to not only cope but rise above your situation.

E is for Exercise.

As I left on my lunchtime run that day, my heart was heavy with the concerns of work. My career had taken me to work I disliked and a boss who was known for his anger. He would get so worked up that foam would form at the corners of his mouth. Running had become my sanctuary, a time when I could escape the pressures of work and find clarity in chaos. Little did I know that on this run, I would stumble upon the answer that would help me rise above my work situation.

As I ran past the two-mile marker, the halfway point of today's four-mile run, my mind flashed back to cross-country in high school. I recalled that in my senior year, I almost didn't qualify for the team. Unlike my previous years, the coach required each of us to qualify for the team. And for me, I wondered whether I'd make the team, as I missed the 26:00 time in my first attempt, clocking a time of over twenty-seven minutes. But there was something different in my second attempt. I had a little more of a spring in my step that day as our group of eight started our run. I remember looking at my watch at the two-mile mark in wonder—12:20, which was thirty seconds better than my goal. I also recall how I led the qualifying race all the way through as I approached the finish line and the coach fumbled around with his stopwatch as I crossed the finish line, presumably because he hadn't expected someone to finish that quickly. I finished with a time of 24:48—two minutes faster than my previous time and a minute faster than my goal.

There was something about that memory and today's run that gave me the courage and fortitude to let go of my work situation and entrust it into God's hands. As I pushed myself up the final hill of the run that day, my eyes filled with tears. To this day, I don't know if I was crying because I had pushed myself so hard that day or whether it was because of the relief from knowing things were going to be alright or both. Honestly, it's the first and only time I remember crying on a run. Again, exercise had given me the mental clarity needed to rise above my work situation. It served as a reminder of my own strength and capability, reinforcing my self-confidence in the face of adversity.

Everything that happened during my run that day was "inner working". My situation at work hadn't changed a bit. The thing that changed was on the inside—my self-confidence and the knowledge that God was going to take care of it.

What I want you to experience and get from this chapter is that the answer to your personal situation resides within: your self-confidence and your connection with God. Going back to the story, later that day I had a brainstorming session with a colleague, and the results of that half-hour meeting was the catalyst that led to one of the most fulfilling positions of my career.

You, too, can experience the same benefits from exercise. By incorporating exercise into your routine, you can not only improve physical fitness, but also fortify your mental and emotional well-being and give clarity to a given situation that you find yourself in. For me, it became a powerful tool that allowed me to rise above the negative effects of workplace bullying, find my voice, and reclaim control over my professional life. If running isn't your thing, pick another form of exercise that you could do by yourself, thinking your own thoughts. Here are a few ideas that have also worked for me and others: 1) hiking 2) a walk 3) biking 4) gardening 5) golfing 6) lawn mowing 7) yoga 8) aerobics. These are just a few things you could do.

M is for Meditation

Volumes could be and have been written about meditation and its benefits. Here I'll limit my discussion to the whys, hows and whats of meditation in the context of bullying, harassment, or conflict.

The Whys of Meditation for Bullying, Harassment, and Conflict

For me, I picked up meditation fifteen years ago through a group that met for meditation in Cincinnati once every couple of weeks. At the time, I practiced some at home but didn't make it a practice. Five years ago, I started meditating regularly again when I found myself in the middle of a workplace bullying situation. Of the bullying/harassment situations I've experienced in my career, this was the most difficult. Daily I thought about leaving my job, but I stuck around because my kids were only a couple of years from graduating from the local high school. In the following ways, meditation was key in helping me to rise above the negativity of that situation, and it can help you rise above yours:

1. **Relax**. At the core of meditation is relaxation. During my bullying situation my mind would be racing for a way out or for solutions to my situation. Meditation helped me give my mind a break from the racing thoughts.
2. **Process emotions**. In the middle of my bullying situation, I was worried about how the bullying was affecting my career and was resentful and angry with my supervisor for using many of the covert bullying tactics brought up in chapter 2. Meditation helped me process my emotions, lowering both the frequency and intensity of my emotions.

3. **Develop resilience and lower stress and anxiety**. Meditation increases awareness of the present moment while simultaneously decreasing surrounding distractions and wandering thoughts. Once I made meditation a daily practice, I was able to carry that meditative state throughout my day. And by tapping into this meditative state throughout my day, I was able to tune out the stress and anxiety related to my bullying situation. In recent years, meditation helped me through one of the more stressful periods of my life—the stresses of Covid followed by my wife having a severe stroke, losing a job and moving across the country.

4. **Added perspective**. Meditation also helped me "get out of myself". There is a practice within meditation called "observing the observer". In this practice, you observe your own thoughts and emotions as they arise without judgment. This practice helped me detach myself from my own emotions and thoughts that arose from the bullying. By applying this practice, I was able to see my situation from more of an outside perspective.

5. **Raise emotional intelligence**. Because "observing the observer" helped me detach from my thoughts and emotions, I was able to

use this practice to raise my emotional intelligence in both aspects brought up in the last chapter:

- raising my emotional regulation and thus keeping my emotions out of discussions with my supervisor
- raising my empathy for others and specifically for my supervisor

11. **Plug into an outside power source**. As an electrical appliance plugs into an outlet and gets electrified, so too has meditation helped me plug in to a power source outside of myself. Some of my greatest thoughts for self-improvement or creative ideas have come from plugging in to God during meditation.

12. **See my true potential**. Meditation helped me detach myself from what I do, seeing myself for that miracle that I am and seeing my true potential. This was one of Jen Sincero's main points in her book, *You Are a Badass: How To Stop Doubting Your Greatness and Start Living an Awesome Life*.

13. **Enhance self-confidence and assertiveness**. Meditation helped me boost my self-confidence and empowered me to assert myself in my workplace bullying situation. Through meditation, you can develop a deeper sense of self-awareness and self-acceptance, which can increase your belief in your own worth and

abilities. This newfound confidence helped me assert my boundaries and stand up to mistreatment.

14. **Get sleep**. Before I started meditation as a practice, I found myself waking up in the middle of the night with my mind racing from the latest round of bullying from the previous day. In some cases, I would lie awake from 3 a.m. until the time I had to get ready for work. Once I started meditation, I was able to put myself back to sleep when I'd wake up in the middle of the night by applying the practices of meditation and relaxation as I lay in bed.

15. **Cultivate gratitude, compassion, love, and forgiveness**. Sometimes it would be before meditation and sometimes afterwards that I would ask for gratitude, compassion, empathy, love, or forgiveness. Workplace bullying can create a hostile environment not only devoid of these positives but exactly the opposite. Meditation can help foster each of these positives first toward oneself and secondly toward others. By practicing meditation and specifically asking for gratitude, compassion, love, and forgiveness, you can cultivate feelings of goodwill and extend them to your bully or harasser. This can promote understanding, and, in my case, it shifted the

dynamics toward a more compassionate and supportive workplace environment.

16. **Cultivate equanimity**. Equanimity is the ability to remain calm and composed in the face of adversity. Meditation practices can strengthen your capacity for equanimity by training you to observe situations without becoming overly reactive or emotionally charged. This can enable you to navigate workplace bullying with a balanced and composed mindset, allowing you to respond thoughtfully rather than react impulsively.

17. **Promote positive mindset and reframing**. Workplace bullying can often lead to negative self-talk and a pessimistic outlook. Meditation can help cultivate a positive mindset by challenging negative thought patterns and promoting self-compassion. Through mindfulness practices, you can learn to reframe negative experiences, develop a more optimistic perspective, and cultivate resilience in the face of adversity.

You, too, can use meditation amid your bullying, harassment, general work conflict, or any other negative situation to rise above and overcome the effects of that situation.

What is Meditation?

Meditation is simply giving your mind a vacation from thinking. If you think about it, our minds are always active. Even as we sleep our mind is active. This is even more the case when you find yourself in the middle of a bullying or harassment situation. Meditation is simply giving your mind a vacation from all of that thinking by tuning in to the present moment.

Hows of meditation

The one phone app that has been most helpful for me in making meditation a habit is simply my alarm and my timer. Setting an alarm for the same time every day as a reminder to begin my meditation and then setting my timer for the duration of my meditation. For your meditation, you want to find a quiet location that will be free of interruptions. This can be a basement, garage, back porch, outbuilding, or bathroom. If you have young children or pets, you want to pick a time when they're away, sleeping, or quiet.

Sit in a comfortable position on a comfortable surface. You can sit with your legs crossed on a mat or in a seated position on a chair, bench, couch, or swing seat. Set your timer for your meditation and sit there tuning in to either your own breath, nature sounds, city sounds, or otherwise. The idea during your meditation is to clear your mind of wandering thoughts. However, if you have thoughts during your meditation, simply let them pass by without judgment like clouds that would pass overhead on a lazy afternoon. When you meditate, it is helpful to close your eyes and focus on your non-visual senses. When I first started meditation, I started with five minutes and worked my way up to ten minutes. Some days, when I have less time, I'll meditate for just two or three minutes. There are no hard and fast rules here on how to do it or how long to do it—this is time for you to take a break from the craziness and busyness of your life.

To help you ease into meditation, I recommend you start with just three to five minutes per day and work your way up to five to ten minutes. As you get good at meditation and see its benefits, you can raise the duration and the frequency. Eventually, you can work your meditation practices into every moment in life (e.g., when you rise in the morning or when you take a shower). You may not be able to close your eyes in every instance (e.g., while driving) but you can practice the other aspects. In fact, during such tasks, you'll find that meditation can enhance any of your daily activities—at work, during exercise, on a hike, during an argument, etc. I believe that meditation can be as powerful a tool as exercise when done as a daily habit.

Meditation References

I recommend that you delve into meditation beyond what I've written here. To find a good read on meditation, plug "meditation book" into Amazon and pick any one of the books that have had both a high number of ratings and the highest ratings. The books that have helped me the most in my personal meditation journey are:

> *Meditation for Busy People* by Osho
> *Inner Engineering: A Yogi's Guide to Joy* by Sadhguru
> *Karma: A Yogi's Guide to Crafting Your Destiny* by Sadhguru

P is for Positivity

Surround yourself with positivity

Surround yourself with positive people. The corollary for this is also true: distance yourself from toxic people where you can. This goes for your home life, school life, as well as your work life. I'll dive into more on how to keep toxicity out of your life in chapter 7 when I discuss creating a safe space for yourself. Think of the individuals in your life—who is the most positive and who is the most supportive of you and your goals? These are the individuals you want to surround yourself with. These are the folks who will always take your side, who always see the good in you and who focus on your best qualities. Spend more time with these individuals—go out to dinner with them, go golfing, etc. Choose activities with these individuals that you know both of you would enjoy.

You being the positivity

Both in your meditations and in your actions, focus on and practice gratitude, generosity, forgiveness, kindheartedness, thankfulness, love, joy, and peace. Think back to my example of Leo Buscaglia in the last chapter. You be Leo Buscaglia in other people's lives. Be the positivity that you desire to see in others. Others will quite often mirror back what they see in us. Put the most effort into being positive in those situations that have the potential to be the most negative. Read the book *How to Win Friends and Influence People* by Dale Carnegie and apply those learnings to your daily life. That book has had such a profound impact on me that I gave it to each of my children and many of the individuals who have worked for me over the years. Ask God for each of these attributes and he'll be faithful in giving them to you.

Affirmations and Prayer

I'm a big believer in the power of our words. And one thing you can do to help yourself in the middle of a work bullying or harassment situation is to use your power of words for good in your situation in the form of "affirmations", or statements that you speak out loud toward the goal of keeping positive. These can help you rise above the situation and give you more power over your situation. Here are some affirmations and prayers that can help you rise above your situation:

a. I am strong and capable of handling this situation with grace and professionalism.

b. I refuse to let the actions of others affect my self-worth, confidence, and joy.

c. I choose to focus on the positive things in my life.

d. I am grateful for _____, _____, and _____. (List out at least three things you're grateful for having in your life.)

e. I have the power to stand up for myself and set boundaries in a respectful manner.

f. I am surrounded by positive energy and support.

g. I am in control of my own actions and emotions, and I will not let the actions of others control my behavior.

h. I choose to respond with kindness and empathy toward those who bully me, as their bullying is a reflection of their own insecurities.

i. I trust my abilities and know that I can achieve success despite the obstacles I face.

j.   I am grateful for this experience as it allows me to grow and become a stronger, more resilient individual.

k.   I am dedicated to my personal success and will work hard to achieve the life I desire.

l.   I surrender the situation into your hands, God, asking that you take up my case and right where I've been wronged.

m. God, I thank you for the maturity you're developing in me through this current situation, ask that you would give me the grace to forgive those who have wronged me, and ask that you show me your path forward to the other side of this negative situation.

n.   I am constantly learning and growing, and each challenge helps me to become a better version of myself.

o.   I am worthy of love and respect and will not settle for anything less.

p.   I choose to focus on the positive aspects of my life.

q.   I am capable of overcoming any obstacle that comes my way.

r.   I will prioritize my personal mental and physical health over my current work situation.

s.   Give me the fortitude to take the actions necessary to set boundaries with my bully (or harasser) and take additional steps as necessary.

t.   Give me a pure heart and right attitude when talking to my bully or harasser.

u.   I am steadfast and resolute in seeing this situation through to closure.

Pick five or more of these affirmations and say them aloud at least twice a day—in the morning and when you return from work as a minimum, but also when you have another encounter with this individual. Write them down on a note card and carry them in your wallet or keep them as a note in your phone, so you're ready to read them out loud in your time of need or otherwise. Go back over this list once every week or two to see if you want to add or substitute one. Add affirmations more specific to your situation using my twenty affirmations as a springboard for your own.

O is for Out - Take a time out

a.   Count to ten in the middle of a situation and don't reply in kind to the negativity of a bully or harasser.

b.   Excuse yourself from a negative situation.

c.   Take a short time between meetings or alone at your desk after finishing tasks.

d.   Take time off by yourself at lunchtime.

e.   Take an afternoon off just for yourself for times when your work is light and do what you would enjoy most if you had time alone to yourself. Some ideas:

    i.   A hike: being alone with nature can be both relaxing and rejuvenating.

    ii.   A hobby that you usually don't have time for (gardening, woodworking, arts and crafts, etc.)

f.   Schedule an outing with your friends (work and/or nonwork). Go to a sporting event or have a spa day or do something completely different like an escape room or axe throwing.

g.   Schedule a vacation. Taking some time off can clear your mind of your current situation. If the stress is enough at work and your finances and work allow, you may want to take a sabbatical— something more like one to six months. Again, your own personal health is a priority over your work. And this is one way to show it to yourself and others.

W is for Welfare – Take Care of Yourself

More important than any other time in your life, you should be taking care of your physical well-being. You need both your strength and health to face the negativity of your situation. Eating right, exercise, and good sleep are all keys toward this goal.

Eat and drink right

This includes both eating foods and consuming drinks that are good for you and avoiding those that are unhealthy. Eat leafy greens, fruits, vegetables, and high protein, low-fat foods. Likewise, lower or eliminate sugary drinks, sugary foods, alcohol, and processed foods.

Exercise

Exercise is not only helpful for your mental well-being and clarity as I pointed out at the beginning of this chapter, it is helpful in your overall health and physical well-being. You'll see in my future book on weight loss that exercise is healthier for you than any supplement or food that you could eat. Exercise itself can reverse aging, fight cancer, undo type 2 diabetes and strengthen your bones and muscles, including your most important muscle, your heart.

Good Sleep

Make sure you get both high quality and the right quantity of sleep. If you have trouble sleeping because of worries connected to the negative situation, practice the relaxation techniques you learn through meditation or breathing exercises or both. If you feel you're not getting enough sleep, you may need to move up the time at which you go to bed. Other ways to increase both the quality and quantity of your sleep:

- Lower or eliminate your alcohol intake.
- Ban pets from your bedroom.
- Use adequate white noise to cover noises outside of your control (a snoring partner or noisy neighbors).
- Block light from your room or your eyes.
- Enhance your sleep environment. This can be through a more straightened room and the addition of an essential oil diffuser.
- Don't look at your phone at any time during the night.
- If you have young children waking you up, research how to get children to sleep through the night and apply those learnings. Avoid "the family bed" for sleep time.
- If you have physical pain waking you up, do what you can to mitigate or eliminate the pain.
- If you have muscle spasms waking you up, then take supplements to reduce these spasms such as magnesium glycinate, vitamin E, vitamin B, and gaba.
- Take sleep enhancing supplements such as melatonin, 5-HTP, chamomile, passionflower, lemon balm and ashwagandha.

The amount and quality of your sleep will affect both your mental as well as physical well-being. And we know from current studies that if you're not getting enough sleep over long periods of time, then you could be building up toxins and plaque within your brain, putting you at a higher risk for Alzheimer's disease (National Institute on Aging). During the REM portion of the sleep cycle, our brains go through a "cleaning cycle" similar to a dishwasher, in which toxins and plaque are removed from the brain, helping us to improve memory and feel refreshed and energetic the next day (J. Hamilton).

E is for Exhale - Deep Breathing Exercises

This can be done at any time and can help you to relax if you're feeling stressed. Deep breathing exercise is nothing more than just taking deep breaths in through your nose and exhaling deep breaths out. Take a deep breath in now for three to five seconds and exhale for three to five seconds. With this one breath cycle, you instantly feel relaxed. Continue this deep breathing for one to five minutes. Your breathing in and out should follow a natural, relaxed flow. It should never be forced. Visualize taking in positivity as you breathe in and letting go of any negative thoughts or emotions as you breathe out. This could be as simple as breathing in peace and calm and breathing out stress and negative emotions. Deep breathing exercises have been shown to relieve stress and have multiple physical benefits associated with the relief of stress. I recommend you go to this resource for more information (Cleveland Clinic).

Practice this while you're at work when you feel the stress or shortly after. Take a personal time out between meetings or between work duties and practice deep breathing exercises. Learning this could be helpful in the middle of your situation. If you're able to find a quiet, remote place between meetings, then you can combine this practice with a two- to five-minute meditation session.

R is for Reverse - Flip the Script

Look at this situation from the angle of personal development. See it as an opportunity to improve instead of the negative situation that it is. By this, I don't mean for you to live in denial with what's going on but instead to take it as an opportunity to become *great*! Take it as an opportunity to learn how to work with difficult people and learn to become a better version of yourself: 1) more resilient 2) more equanimous 3) more self-aware. All of the Greatest Of All Times (GOATs) in history had to first go through the valley before getting to the mountaintop. Here is just a short list of these greats and their valley:

- Michael Jordan, considered to be the greatest basketball player of all time was cut from his high school varsity basketball team in his sophomore year. (Piccotti)

- Tom Brady, considered to be the football GOAT, was the eleventh quarterback picked and the 199th overall pick in the sixth round of the 2000 NFL draft. (Mel Kiper Jr.) (Biography.com)
- Albert Einstein felt alienated in elementary school, struggled with typical classroom learning, had speech challenges and, when he came of military age, dropped out of school to avoid the draft. (Tyler Piccotti)
- Henry Ford's first attempts at an automobile business failed. (Biography.com)
- Thomas Edison's teachers labeled him as a difficult student because he was hyperactive and easily distracted. (Biography.com)
- J.K. Rowling was a single mom living off welfare when she wrote her first Harry Potter novel, and her first Harry Potter book was rejected multiple times before she found a publisher. (Biography.com) (Ree Hines)
- Dr. Seuss had his first book rejected by twenty-sven publishers. (Andrew)
- Ghandi struggled with insecurities as a teenager to the point that he slept with the lights on. He rebelled against his parents' religion, eating meat, smoking, and stealing change from household servants. Later, as a lawyer, he blanked out in his first courtroom

case. He later in life became a prominent figure in India's independence movement and addressed racism through peaceful means in South Africa and India. This later became a blueprint for peaceful civil activism that Martin Luther King and Nelson Mandella adopted. (Biography.com)

- Walt Disney went bankrupt with his first cartoon business and was rejected by 300 banks when trying to finance his Mickey Mouse cartoon. (Pak)
- After a small movie role, an executive told Harrison Ford he'd never succeed as an actor. (Biography.com)
- Oprah Winfrey was fired from her first television job because she was "too emotionally invested in her stories". (Ward)
- Billy Joel's first album underperformed in its first fifteen weeks after release, nearly sinking him as a performing artist. (Yates)
- Lady Gaga was dropped by her recording label, Def Jam, after three months. (Biography.com)
- Steven Spielberg was rejected by the University of Southern California School of Cinematic Arts multiple times. (McBride)

What was it that helped the GOATs to ignore the naysayers and failures to achieve their goals?

The answer:

1. **Clear, Achievable Vision.** Each of these GOATs had a clear vision of their success and believed they could achieve it.

2. **Stick-to-itiveness**. Each GOAT had the determination to succeed, and their determined attitude carried them through setbacks or failures. In fact, many of them viewed setbacks or failures as stepping stones to reach their goals. Edison said, "I have not failed 10,000 times, I've successfully found 10,000 ways that will not work." (Hendry)

3. **Self-actualization**. The closer the GOATs came to their goals, the easier it was for them to see themselves achieving their goals. This is a similar concept to the story of *The Little Engine That Could* by Watty Piper, where the closer the engine came to the apex of the hill, the more the engine believed that they could meet their goal of overcoming the hill.

4. **Building on Success**. Not only did the GOATs view failure differently, but they took their successes and continued to build one success upon the other. Each success became a splash of color on the canvas of their life until the finished product stood there before us all to admire.

Let this be the same for you. Follow the blueprint to greatness shown by these GOATs. Remember that before these GOATs were great, they were ordinary people like you and me. Flip the script on your bullying, harassment, or conflict situation. Imagine achieving your goal and go out and start working toward achieving it. Let any bullying, harassment, naysayers, or failures motivate you more toward achieving your goals. The GOATs did.

See your greatness! You're going through your valley on your way to greatness.

Pulling it All Together

Each of the elements that make up the word EMPOWER can help you to not only deal with but rise above your situation. Regardless of whether it's a bullying situation, harassment situation, or general work conflict, you not only got this, but this is your springboard to launching your best life. You are an amazing and talented person—your mountaintop awaits you.

Chapter 6 Homework

1. Write out the elements that make up the acronym for EMPOWER.

    E_____

    M_____

    P_____

    O_____

    W_____

    E_____

    R_____

2. Rate the above from one to ten in the space next to each word in #1 above, where one stands for "I'm currently not doing" and ten stands for "I'm doing this currently and it's currently a daily habit of mine".

3. Choose three of the EMPOWER elements that you think would benefit you the most by improving or making into a daily habit. List these three elements here in order of priority with #1 being your top priority to make into a daily habit.

    1. _____

    2. _____

    3. _____

4. Next to each of these elements that you want to improve, write an action that will help you toward making this a daily habit.

5. Write these three actions on your calendar for next week starting on Monday and fill these actions in for your next month.

6. Do these daily actions on each day that you've written down.

7. One week before the following month, fill in these actions to that month's calendar.

8. Do these daily actions next month. Continue doing this routine monthly of filling in your calendar the week before the next month and doing those actions daily in that month following your calendar.

CHAPTER 7

SAFE SPACE

A s he sat by the babbling brook, the soothing sound of the water provided temporary relief from the whirlwind of thoughts weighing heavily on him. He always looked forward to this part of his week when he would pull over to the small park on his drive back to his Dearborn office from the plant where the door trim panels were manufactured. His thoughts volleyed between the meeting he had just left and his wife at home on bedrest. Labor had begun unexpectedly a few weeks before, after a placental abruption. If the baby had been born that day, it would be born three months early, putting the baby's life at risk.

His mind returned to the problem he was working through at work: how can we reproduce the failure that our customers are seeing in the field quickly and repeatably? Failed door trim panels were being returned without explanation. Was it due to normal customer use, customer abuse, a manufacturing issue, a design issue, or was it some combination of some or all of these?

But there was another concern gnawing at him—the team leader he had to work with. Her temper and impatience were legendary within the team. In moments of frustration, she resorted to yelling, cursing, and berating her colleagues, leaving them demoralized. The memory of her explosive outburst, when she physically confronted him, grabbing him by the collar and berating him for a delayed test, replayed in his mind vividly. Her behavior was unacceptable, creating a toxic work environment that hindered collaboration and productivity.

As the babbling brook continued its gentle flow, he contemplated the significance of these three challenges. The health and well-being of his wife and unborn baby being his top concern, pushing him to prioritize family above all else. Simultaneously, the need to address the workplace issues became increasingly evident. The team's cohesion and morale were at stake, and the toxic behavior of the team leader needed to be addressed.

In this moment of reflection, the babbling brook acted as a source of solace, allowing him to gather his thoughts and find clarity. The serenity of the natural surroundings reminded him of the importance of finding balance between his personal and professional life. With renewed determination, he resolved to address the workplace challenges head-on, seeking a resolution that would foster a healthier, more collaborative work environment.

Leaving the babbling brook behind, he returned to his responsibilities, armed with a newfound sense of purpose. As he navigated the complexities of his work and personal life, he understood that finding solutions required both inner strength and the support of those around him. With this realization, he embarked on a path toward resolution, determined to overcome the obstacles before him and create a better future for himself, his family, and his colleagues.

This is a story that took place over twenty-five years ago for me. And I use it now to illustrate the importance of finding and creating a safe space for yourself. The pressures of both work and home life can be overwhelming especially when "the planets align" and all of the stresses at home and at work occur together. This story also highlights the importance of having empathy for our work colleagues who carry untold, underlying home and work stresses and anxieties.

Creating a "Safe Space" for Yourself

As I write this section, I just saw the neighbor's cat lying in the sun on our small deck adjacent to our kitchen, and I pondered, "Why does the cat like to come over here?" Almost as soon as I thought the question, the answer came to me: "Because it's a safe space". The neighbor's yard has two young golden retriever puppies who are very playful and chase the cat as their favorite pastime. And the cat comes over here to lie on our porch and relax, away from the dogs who stay in the neighbor's yard because of an invisible fence. And so it is with you. You, in your harassment or bullying situation, need a safe place.

A Safe Place Away From the Bully or Harasser

If the world was optimized for preventing workplace harassment and bullying, you could snap your fingers and you would no longer have to work with the bully or harasser—or at least you'd get moved to a different building. And like the neighbor's cat sleeping on my deck, you could be somewhere else, in a more relaxed situation. Unfortunately, in the real world, work conflicts will take much longer than a snap of the fingers to resolve. In time, the harassers and bullies of my past moved on. But it was only after other steps had taken place. Until those other steps take place, you can create your own safe space. It is okay to limit your interactions with the bully or harasser. And if the person is a harasser and they harass you again, then it's okay for you to get up and walk away without explanation.

A Physical Safe Space

Because working remotely has become more common in recent years, working from home may be an acceptable solution to bullying or harassment. If it's a harassment situation, then working remotely can bring your interactions with the harasser closer to zero. If it's a bullying situation and your manager is the bully, then you will have to limit interactions and respectfully set boundaries to create a safe space.

You should also consider finding a quiet, remote place away from work, where you can think your own thoughts and process your emotions as I did in my story at the beginning of this chapter. If your quiet remote place has running water, as mine did, you'll get the added benefits that running water brings, as running water triggers the parasympathetic nervous system. And if you can't find a quiet place nearby that has running water, download and play an app that has the sounds of running water.

A Mental Safe Space

Create a safe space for yourself in your mind. This can be done using the same tools of meditation that I introduced earlier. You should have at least one set time each day where you meditate, whether that's before work, at your lunch break, or after work. Try to incorporate the state of meditation throughout your day, applying mindfulness as part of your pre- and post-meeting routine—even if it's for fifteen to thirty seconds.

A Safe Space via Self-Advocacy

You can create a safe space for yourself by respectfully setting boundaries with the bully or harasser. Again, there is no better advocate for you than you. The effectiveness of this boundary-setting is dependent on your own assertiveness, confidence, and poise when meeting with your bully or harasser.

Assertiveness Techniques and Establishing Boundaries

When my kids were younger, I would stop at the Starbucks Coffee shop in the Center Circle of Indianapolis enroute to my parents' house. On one such occasion, I told my kids before going in that, if they wanted something, they'd have to place their own order. After waiting twenty minutes in line, I thought we had all gotten what we wanted as we exited the coffee shop. As I looked, I noticed that everyone had coffee and a treat in hand except one—and the one who had nothing had crocodile tears welling in her eyes. I asked what had happened and apparently, the cashier had asked what I wanted (I was in line in front of this daughter) and then took the order of the person behind her without even asking her what she wanted. I had a good talk with her back then, letting her know that she needs to speak up for herself—to self-advocate. She probably is the closest in personality to me; when I was her age, I would have likely done the same thing if someone skipped me in line. If you're like me and speaking up for yourself is a challenge or you're used to putting the needs of others ahead of your own needs, then utilizing assertiveness techniques can be very helpful for you.

Assertiveness techniques can help you to better represent yourself, making sure that your needs are heard and met. You may need to learn and apply assertiveness techniques if:

- You handle conflict with avoidance or appeasement. Look at how you've addressed conflict in your past. Be honest with yourself. If your go-to method for conflict resolution is either conflict avoidance or appeasing others, then you need to practice some assertiveness techniques.
- Others think you could benefit from assertiveness. Ask work friends, family, or nonwork friends what their perception is of your level of assertiveness. If you want to see what people really think, do it as an anonymous survey through an app like SurveyMonkey. See if your own personal rating differs from the

ratings that others have given you. If it's different, then, again, you'll need to incorporate assertiveness techniques.

Assertive communication. Assertive communication is basically just standing up for yourself. If you don't like something, then simply tell the person, "I don't like such and such." When you speak for yourself, you don't have to raise your voice and you don't have to show anger. In fact, if you have anger, you probably want to wait until you're no longer angry to express yourself. One time a colleague came up behind me in my cubicle and pinned my head to my desk—for roughly a minute. As you can imagine, when he finally let go, I was angry. But I didn't want to retaliate so I kept what I said brief and to the point. In less than a minute I had him out of my office and went directly to my boss's office and asked him what he thought should be done. At my boss's recommendation, I scheduled a one-on-one meeting later with this guy and calmly told him that his harassment had to stop. If you find yourself, as I did, in a potentially charged situation, then you should wait until you've cooled down to address it as I did.

Practice assertive communication. Your words should be clear, direct, and respectful. You should stand up for yourself, but do so without being aggressive. Write out key points that you want to communicate to a bully or harasser. At a minimum, you want to cite the behavior that bothers you and tell them how it makes you feel. Be prepared with a response for the bully or harasser if they make excuses or blame you. If there is something on your end that you need to apologize for, do so genuinely and up front. By yourself, practice what you're going to say and later, role play standing up for yourself with a friend, family member, or significant other. Switch roles and you play the bully or harasser to see how the other person would respond. Pay close attention to not only what they say, but their body language. Does the tone of their voice and body language exude confidence and assertiveness or the opposite? Incorporate what you like and avoid what you don't like from your observations.

Let your body do the talking. There's an old story from early US history where Gouverneur Morris took a dare from Alexander Hamilton to slap George Washington on the shoulder during the 1787 Constitutional Convention in Philadelphia. Mr. Morris took the bet and put his hand on Washington's shoulder and said, "My dear general, I am very happy to see you look so well!". Washington, in turn, stepped back and basically gave him a silent stare until Morris retreated into the crowd (Bell). Washington had let his body do the talking. So it should be for you also to let your body do the talking— speaking confidence and poise. Harness your inner George Washington using your body language to speak the unspoken—that you won't tolerate bullying or harassment. Keep direct eye contact, upright and confident posture, and use the pregnant pause as Washington did.

Practice in front of a mirror. By yourself, practice what you're going to say in front of a mirror. Look for and apply the following Do's and avoid the following Don'ts:

Do's:

- Keep eye contact.
- Keep your posture upright and looking engaged.
- Have a relaxed and confident facial expression.
- If you speak, use direct and firm language.
- Use confident body language.
- Practice and get comfortable with the pregnant pause.

Don'ts:

- Slouch
- Use filler sounds, words, or phrases such as "like", "um", "er", or "you know what I'm saying"
- Smile
- Be tense, aggressive, or emotional

The more you practice, the better you'll get at being assertive. The phrase "Fake it till you make it" applies to raising your self-confidence, which will feed your assertiveness. How do you get more confident and assertive? Practice, practice, practice. And the more confidence and respectful assertiveness you exude, the less likely you'll be bullied or harassed in the future.

Summary

It's important to your health to find and create safe spaces for yourself. Safe spaces will contribute to both your mental and physical well-being, giving you a respite from bullying or harassment. You are your best advocate and by learning and applying the assertiveness and confidence techniques outlined in this chapter, you can raise how others see you, potentially preventing future bullying or harassment.

Chapter 7 Homework

1. Name the three ways given in this chapter for creating a safe space.

   _____ -

   _____ -

   _____ -

1. After each item listed above, identify actions to create safe spaces for yourself in each of these areas.

2. Practice in front of a mirror the "Do's" and "Don'ts" of assertiveness given in the chapter, pretending to be in a real life situation where you need to use assertiveness.

3. Use your assertiveness technique in a real life situation at work or in your personal life.

CHAPTER 8

TRAINING: KEY CATALYST FOR CULTURAL IMPROVEMENT

As I mentioned in chapter 5, I was assigned to lead a Navy-wide tiger team that was to address the very issue that had ignited my colleague in the story of chapter 1. Prior to leading this tiger team, I took a course on brainstorming that taught key tools in brainstorming, effective meeting facilitation, and how to harness the power of opposing opinions within a team. And I saw firsthand the value of training as I used the freshly learned brainstorming tools to fuel team collaboration. And now, having been a trainer myself for the past twelve years, I've personally seen the value of training from the other side. In the context of bullying, harassment, and conflict, training can be that tool that helps individuals and organizations work and play well together, fostering a productive, creative, and innovative work environment.

Optimally, training should be more proactive and less reactive, where proactive training is training that would occur before negative conflict situations arise, and reactive training is training after harassment, bullying, or conflict has occurred. Because this book is written for those already in a negative situation, I'll give a high-level view of proactive training and do a deeper dive into reactive training.

The training in this chapter is by no means an exhaustive list. It is simply a list of training that can be helpful to prevent or mitigate harassment, bullying, and conflict. The following are just a few benefits I've seen that training can have over the knowledge gained from reading a book:

- You're able to ask questions specific to your situation.
- You have accountability to your teachers and fellow students in your knowledge, understanding, and application of the topics taught.
- The trainer can emphasize the points through various forms of media and examples.
- A course can test your understanding of topics and their applicability to you with quizzes and tests.

- The concepts can be reenforced through practice via workshops where you apply what you've learned.

Proactive Training

Proactive training should be taught at a level of awareness for everyone in a given organization and at an advanced level for those who are part of the leadership team.

Awareness training for everyone should include:

- Culture of not only acceptance but believing in and inspiring one another
- Corporate definitions of harassment, bullying, and general conflict
- Awareness of good and bad behaviors for conflict resolution
- Individual and organizational benefits of good conflict resolution behaviors
- Individual and organizational harms of bad conflict resolution behaviors
- How each of us has a role in preventing harassment and bullying
- Covert and overt forms of harassment and bullying
- The process elements and steps that make up RECTIFY in chapter 3

- Conflict resolution and the elements of PEACE in chapter 5
- Review of company policies regarding harassment, bullying, and conflict resolution

Leadership Training

Strong, Effective, Supportive, Protective, and Inspiring Leadership. The good and the bad of an organization's culture rests upon the attributes of that organization's leadership team. Because a given leadership team comes from a variety of life and work experiences, leadership training is an essential first step toward developing leadership qualities necessary for a productive and innovative work culture. The best way to prevent the negatives associated with bullying and harassment is to first train the positives that are the antithesis of these negatives. This training will focus on getting the most from your team using positive qualities in leadership, and motivating your team by methods that inspire which are diametrically opposed to the methods employed in covert bullying. The following are foundational elements for good leadership development training:

- **Supporting and believing in your team members.** In such training, leaders are taught the value of getting the best performance from the team members by believing in them. Why? Go back to the GOATs of chapter 6. What was it that helped them to become the GOATs? Answer: they first believed in themselves. If you want a team of GOATs, you must first believe in them, thus imparting "belief in them." An organization that believes in one another will often outperform organizations with more talent that employ bullying techniques.

Jimmy Valvano demonstrated the power of this concept through his coaching and expressed it in his speech entitled, "The Gift My Father Gave Me". The gift that Jimmy is referring to in this speech is his dad's unwavering belief that his son was going to win the NCAA March Madness basketball tournament. And in 1983, Jimmy's North Carolina State team did the improbable—by not only winning their first-round game, but by winning the next three games to make it to the Final Four. Then they faced Georgia, who had just beaten their more talented neighbors, North Carolina, who had sophomore guard Michael Jordan and had won the tournament the previous year. NC State, being the lowest seed left in the Final Four that year, was given less than 5 percent chance of winning the tournament. And yet, they not only beat Georgia but beat the heavily favored number 1 overall seed that year, Houston. Jimmy's team won that year because he had applied and passed along the gift of believing in others to his team. He told them that they could win, they believed him, and they won.

- **Foster an environment without fear**. Inherent in the concept of believing in others is also the concept of allowing them to make mistakes and allowing them to fail. This is a concept that Dr. Deming had taught to the Japanese that they took to heart, as it's a hallmark of Japanese industrial culture today as part of their Kaizen (continuous improvement) (D. Deming) (Aguayo). I believe this concept was embraced more by Japanese companies than American companies because, prior to Deming, the Japanese culture had already embraced the concept of imperfection through the worldview of Wabi-sabi (Crossley-Baxter). In Japan's Kaizen (continuous improvement) mistakes are okay, and honesty is not only encouraged, but rewarded (Hwang). Organizations that don't encourage and reward honest assessments will be organizations that are more likely to hide or cover mistakes or shortcomings and prevent the organization from a true understanding of where opportunities for improvement are. When this is part of a work culture, an organization will have some amount of fear, which will prevent the full story from being told to the leadership team. And without a clear understanding of the problems, an organization will gloss over problems and thus never fix them.

- **Self-awareness.** Employ leadership self-awareness tools, such as the Johari Window (Shapiro, Heil and Hager) to help each leader "get outside of themselves". Using such tools can help leaders identify and eliminate personal biases.

- **Situational Leadership Model** (Kenton). Individualizing management approach to the needs of the given team or team member. For example, a leader should adjust their level of oversight to the experience level of the employee. An experienced employee will require less oversight than a new employee. An experienced employee could see too much oversight as micromanagement and covert bullying whereas a new employee could see this same level of oversight as necessary and very helpful.

- **Empowering and delegation.** Give each team member autonomy and empower them to make decisions and take ownership of their work. When appropriate, teach leaders to share and delegate their leadership responsibilities.

Other cultural catalysts. Other leadership skills that can help develop team members and optimize their performance:

- Regular constructive feedback in effective one-on-ones
- Recognizing and appreciating achievements
- Challenging teams to hit stretch goals but not frustrating them with unrealistic goals
- The importance of team retreats and team building exercises toward building teams that play well together so they work well together
- The importance of collaboratively developing a mission statement and vision with their team
- Promoting team members based on their merits and independent of personal biases
- Fostering a sense of team and doing things that feed team chemistry
- Assess and leverage strengths of team members
- Assess the personality of the leader and each team member to better understand the role that personality differences play in team dynamics, chemistry, and potential conflicts
- Having positive thoughts and expectations for each member of the team
- Set team members up for success by leveraging their strengths

Other elements that should be taught to leaders proactively regarding conflict resolution and prevention of bullying and harassment are as follows:

- All the elements of the previously mentioned awareness level training
- Leadership level training for identifying and mediating bullying, harassment, and conflict
- Awareness and prevention of covert bullying. Organizational leadership is in a unique position to create an environment free of covert bullying by first understanding what covert bullying is (awareness) and secondly refraining from using these techniques (prevention). In such training the leadership team would be introduced to covert bullying techniques listed in chapter 2, and, second, be encouraged to set the example as leaders by avoiding these methods. Dispel the false pretense that these methods are okay if they work, and encourage, instead, the use of the effective and inspiring leadership elements previously listed under Leadership Training.

If your current organization doesn't include this type of training for individuals or leadership, then your organization has missed the opportunity to train their teams proactively to work well together. Laying this foundation will be helpful in creating a positive work environment that fosters team chemistry, productivity, creativity, and innovation. Lastly, laying this groundwork can prevent and mitigate the negative effects of bullying, harassment, and dysfunctional conflict resolution techniques.

Reactive Training – For Bullying, Harassment, and General Conflict

Reactive training is training that takes place after a work situation has arisen. This training can give a step improvement to any situation, shifting the narrative for all parties involved in conflict and thus improving the overall well-being of an organization's culture. For bullying, harassment, or general work conflict situations, training needs to be targeted to the given situation. If you're a bullied or harassed employee, then the training below can be helpful for you to rise above your situation but shouldn't be mandated. You didn't ask to be bullied or harassed and so you shouldn't be compelled to take this training. In the case of the harasser or bully, the training should be mandatory and should address the root cause of the bullying or harassment situation. The manager of the bully or harasser and the human resource representative should work together toward choosing the training that's appropriate for the given circumstance.

I've classified reactive training into four major categories in this chapter:

- For the bullied or harassed
- For the bully
- For the harasser
- For general conflict

Training for The Target of Harassment or Bullying

Assertiveness. If your personality is timid, reserved, or introverted, then you should consider this type of training. If you find yourself placating others or avoiding conflict, this would be great training for you so you can better advocate for yourself. In such a course, you would be taught the tenets of what I taught in the last chapter toward creating a safe space for yourself.

Self-care. This is a more general category of training for more specific activities that could include any type of training where you're prioritizing your self-improvement—internally, personally, or professionally. The following are just a few examples:

Meditation. I already brought up the benefits of meditation so won't repeat them here; a class would allow you to participate with others and would keep you accountable to the practice of meditation until it becomes a habit. The leader of your meditation can introduce you to principles of meditation, methods to meditate and guide you through topics. Also in a classroom setting, the leaders will often allow the participants to share their personal experiences and specific examples of how the practice of meditation outside the class is helping them. It is likely that you can find a free offering of guided meditation in your community as I did near the University of Cincinnati campus, a group that meets virtually via a free online meditation group.

Physical fitness. Back in the '80s and '90s, the workout classes were limited to aerobics or yoga. Today there are so many options for workout classes—spinning, aerobics, Zumba, Pilates, Barre, TRX, CrossFit, HIIT workouts, etc. The benefits of a physical fitness class are that it offers the benefits of social interaction, body strengthening, and accountability. And the exercise itself has the benefit of clearing your mind in the same way that meditation can.

Mind-Body Technique Class. Yoga, tai chi or qinggong are examples of these. These are the combination of mindfulness that meditation offers with physical activity. Also, meditation itself can be combined with other physical activities like walking, hiking, running, rowing, or biking.

Self-Compassion or Self-Esteem Training. This is another form of training for someone who has lived a life of putting others before themselves or for someone who suffered from mental or physical abuse in their past. If you find yourself putting others' needs or opinions ahead of your own, this would be great training for you, helping you develop the practice of making yourself a priority. Again, your best advocate for you is YOU—such a course will focus on areas that will raise your self-esteem and self-confidence toward making you an even better advocate for yourself.

Time-Management and Boundary-Setting. This is another form of training where you put yourself first. At first, these two may seem unrelated, but time is your greatest commodity and realizing that is your first step toward realizing that others—in the workplace and your personal life—can "steal" this great commodity—time. Creating healthy boundaries with others is the point of this type of training, which is yet another way of putting yourself first.

Nature Therapy. Hiking with a group at a set time at a regular cadence can be therapeutic and give you the accountability and social aspect that a fitness class can offer.

Affirmation Training. Training that focuses on the positive of you. Looking at the power of words and your own imagination to see the greatness within you.

Hobby-related. Any class in a hobby you enjoy or something that you've wanted to try can have both a positive social aspect as well as being cathartic. The following is just a short list of ideas that would fit this category:

- Art Class – Any form of art, whether painting, sculpting, pottery, or some sort of crafting.
- Music Class – This could be learning to play an instrument, furthering your abilities in an instrument you're already familiar with, learning a new instrument, singing, or music appreciation.
- Nutrition Course – What you eat plays a significant role in your personal health, physically and mentally. Taking such a course can improve your knowledge in a topic that can have real, lasting repercussions on your overall well-being and longevity.
- Industrial Arts Class – If your jam is working with wood or home improvement projects or you'd like them to be, then take a class in that interest.
- Cooking Class – Cooking as an art has grown in our society and is a good way to improve your culinary tastes and prowess.
- Gardening – taking a course can help you improve your green thumb or, if you haven't gardened before, can give you the general knowledge to garden. If you don't have a lot of yard space, then experiment with square-foot gardening.

Conflict Resolution. Taking a course on conflict resolution can give you the skills to work through difficult situations or work with difficult people.

Resilience Training. Resilience is your tolerance for stress. Given that the workplace can be a stressful environment at times, this type of training can give you strategies to improve your tolerance for stress in the workplace and in your home life.

Support Group. Meeting with others who have been bullied or harassed in the workplace or home life can be therapeutic.

Brainstorming. As I pointed out in the conflict resolution chapter and earlier in this chapter, brainstorming can be that tool that helps you find multiple solutions to some of the most difficult of situations, helping individuals with opposing thoughts find a solution or multiple solutions that get them to win-win scenarios.

For a Workplace Harasser

Anti-harassment training. Most adults should know what's acceptable behavior in the workplace. However, not everyone enters the workforce with the same level of social skills, and some pick up bad habits from toxic work environments of their past. Think back to my original example that I led the book off with—the culture of the program office beginning each meeting by shouting at and humiliating the other side. Also think back to my example of the team leader who had come up through the plants—she had the habit of using anger and threats as a tool to "get the job done" because "it had always worked in the past". So some training requires first the awareness of what harassment and bullying are and, second, how to stop it in the future, especially for those who have developed and fostered it into habits, considering it "business as usual."

Training to review the company's policies on harassment. If this isn't mandatory training in your workplace, it should be. It's in the best interest of the employees and the employer to have an environment of inclusion and positivity. An organization that "plays well together, works well together". All of the great things that an organization or company wants (productivity, creativity, innovation, and new ideas) require a positive and inclusive environment.

Diversity training. If the harassment was directed at someone in a protected class, then the harasser or bully will need diversity training.

Conflict resolution. If the harassment arose from a work conflict, then conflict resolution training should be in order.

For a Workplace Bully (manager)

Many of the tools that are taught proactively to prevent bullying will need to be retaught reactively if a manager is found to be using overt or covert bullying. The following training should be given to a manager using bullying:

Anti-bullying training. As I pointed out in the A-Z of covert bullying in chapter 2, these forms of bullying can be more subtle because they are less detectable, likely going under the radar of the organization and management above this employee. Covert bullying, however, can be more damaging than overt bullying as it can go on undetected for a long time. And a bully with this type of behavior can get promoted despite this bad behavior, thus casting a wider net of those impacted by their bullying behavior. So it's important that organizations employ ways of detecting these forms of covert bullying and retrain managers who employ such methods.

Diversity training. If the bullying is toward a protected class, then diversity training should be in order.

Leadership development training. As discussed earlier, not only should a manager be taught to avoid the negatives via anti-bullying training, but they should also be taught the positives via leadership development training. Leadership development training will give the tools to managers and directors to model the positivity and inclusivity that they desire to see throughout their organization. Every leader wants to get the best work out of their organization; this training will give them tools to inspire their organization into their greatest work, productivity, creativity, and innovation. This training will help the leader to understand and focus on the strengths of every individual and tailor their management to leverage those strengths.

Personality training. Many conflicts arise because of differences in personalities. By proactively teaching how personality differences can drive differences in how we perceive our work and work goals, potential conflicts arising from personality differences can be understood, mitigated, and averted. As part of this training, the leader or potential leader can take a personality assessment themselves and be taught how that can influence their view of someone having a similar personality vs. those having an opposite personality. The end goal would be to help your organization's leadership treat everyone equally—even those with opposite personalities.

Conflict awareness and resolution training. In this training, a leader is taught the conflict awareness and resolution techniques that I brought up in chapter 5 titled Conflict Resolution. Anyone who is in a manager or other leadership role will likely encounter conflict on a regular basis. Knowing their personal style of conflict resolution and the style of others will help them better deal with personal conflict they encounter as well as rectify conflict between those who work for them and others. Remember from the conflict resolution chapter that healthy, effective conflict resolution will promote the productivity and innovation that you desire as a leader. Likewise, the corollary also holds: negative conflict resolution techniques (e.g., conflict avoidance or "bulldozing") fosters negative work behaviors like many of the covert and overt bullying techniques listed A-Z in chapter 2.

Strengths training. Each individual in an organization comes with their own unique strengths. Strengths training and assessments can help a leader understand their own strengths as well as the strengths of those in their group. In such training, the manager and direct reports can learn what their own personal strengths are with the goal of leveraging and optimizing those strengths within the context of the work that needs to be done by that group. A group that focuses on the strengths of each individual will maximize both team chemistry and productivity.

Self-awareness training. A bully employing the more subtle forms of bullying may be lacking in self-awareness. As mentioned earlier, Johari window can be used as a workshop to determine the amount of self-awareness that an individual has. The Johari window was developed by psychologists Joseph Luft and Harry Ingham in 1955 at the University of California (Shapiro, Heil and Hager) to determine our self-disclosure, self-awareness, approachability, and how we perceive ourselves vs. how others perceive us. The greater the difference between our perception of ourselves and how others perceive us, the lower our self-awareness. Likewise, the more our self-awareness aligns with others' perceptions of us, the greater our self-awareness. I've used this tool in my leadership development training with great success. If an individual is already a manager of people, then the Johari window workshop is the most effective when that individual's direct report's assessment of the leader is with the manager's self-assessment.

Situational leadership training (Kenton). If a leader's management style is the same for every person who works for them regardless of their team's needs, then the leader would benefit from situational leadership training. As mentioned earlier, this type of training teaches a management style that is tailored to the needs of the given team member(s). For example, using a more "hands off" approach for established employees and more "hands on" approach to early career employees, essentially optimizing and tailoring your management to the needs of the employee. In this type of management, an established employee not only doesn't require the day-to-day management approach but is even more productive in a "hands off" approach.

When the Source of Conflict is General Conflict

A human resource representative or some other outside or independent agent to the situation between a manager and an employee can assess the source of the disharmony. Training can be targeted based upon that independent agent's assessment. If the root cause of this disharmony is thought to be a difference in work goals, personalities, or some other difference between the two employees, then training can be assigned to both, targeting the suspected root cause. The following are just a few types of training that could be employed when general conflict arises:

Personality Assessment - If most of the conflict is thought to be the result of personality differences, then a personality assessment given to both employees can be extremely helpful. If, for instance, the manager is more of an "analytic" personality and values the details of their day-to-day work, and the person working for them is more a "visionary" in their personality, then not only will their day-to-day work priorities be different, but how they see and approach life and work will be different. The more visionary personality will talk about work in more general terms and look at the bigger picture. Whereas the person with an analytic personality will see the details in life as being a priority and important. A personality assessment class could help these two employees see that their differences are rooted in their personality differences. The analytic manager (in this example) could resent that the visionary employee doesn't seem to value the details of their work. And they could give the visionary-personality employee negative ratings and feedback because they feel their work priorities are not what they should be. The outputs from such a class as this would be:

- An awareness of their differences
- A better understanding of how the other person thinks
- Why the other person's work priorities are different than their own

Strengths assessment.

Taking an assessment or course on strengths can be another way of seeing each other's differences. Like the personality assessment class, this can help two different employees better understand each other. And what is a better way of understanding each other's differences than focusing on the strengths of the other person.

Conflict resolution training.

Workplace conflict, low-key harassment and low-key bullying can overlap. In some cases, it will likely be difficult for even a professional Human Resource representative to distinguish. Conflict resolution training can introduce and teach two parties involved in workplace conflict to have more healthy responses to workplace conflict regardless of the root cause of the conflict and regardless of whether it's general workplace conflict, bullying, or harassment. The two individuals don't necessarily have to be in the same class. And a class on conflict resolution will likely include workshops with role-playing, helping individuals apply what they're taught in the class.

Recap

I added a whole chapter on training because training is a level above reading a book, as training will not only teach concepts but include workshops to practice what you learn. Choosing training is another way of putting yourself first and flipping the script on your situation, making it about your own personal development.

Chapter 8 Homework

1. Review the training options for targets of harassment or bullying.

   a. From the list of training for targets, find and schedule a course that you think you would benefit from the most.

   b. From the list of training for targets, select and schedule two other training options for yourself to attend in a future year. If you have a personal development plan, add this training to that plan.

CHAPTER 9

SEEKING A PROFESSIONAL

When to Seek the Help of a Professional

Answer yes or no to each of the following questions regarding your work conflict, harassment, or bullying situation:

- Do you regularly think of your work situation at home?
- Has your work situation caused you to lose sleep in the last month?
- Have you thought of getting a new job or explored other work in the last month because of your work situation?
- Do you feel your mental and/or physical well-being have been impacted by your situation?
- Is your work situation too much for you to bear alone?

If you answered yes to one or more of the above questions, then you should reach out for help from a professional. Each question you answered "yes" above indicates your situation is too much and a professional could help you identify, navigate, and overcome the bullying or harassment you're receiving. If you are asking yourself if you should get help, then you probably should have gotten help already. It's human nature to want to work though issues on your own. And in some family upbringings, we've been wrongly taught:

- To bottle our feelings
- To "pull ourselves up by our bootstraps", resolving issues on our own
- That professional help is a sign of weakness

Nothing could be further from the truth. Seeking the help of a professional is a sign of self-awareness and a sign of strength. Honestly, if you bought this book to help yourself through a work or home situation, then you've already reached the point of needing a professional.

Why See a Professional

Whether it's a life coach, therapist, counselor, pastor, or some other professional, the help of someone who has been trained and is practiced at helping others through conflict is exactly what you need. Professional counselors have helped individuals like yourself to identify, navigate, and overcome both home life and/or work conflict.

What a Professional Can Do for You

A professional can help you see your situation from yet another perspective than a coworker, family member, friend, or HR representative. A professional can help you in ways that friends and coworkers can't. They can help by giving you:

- More independent assessment and evaluation of your specific situation at work toward
  - Identifying whether it's bullying/harassment or just general conflict
  - Helping you to discover the root cause of the problem. Knowing the root cause of a problem can help you come up with better, more targeted solutions
  - Weigh the pros and cons of the situation and help you make a better decision on whether to stay with or leave your current employer
  - Evaluate how the situation is affecting your mental and physical well-being
- Come up with a plan of strategies and actions specific to resolving your situation.

- o Helping you with assertiveness if that's not your strong suit toward helping you become your best advocate in a respectful manner
- o Helping you practice setting firm boundaries with your harasser, bully, or coworker that the conflict is with
- o Identify colleagues at work who can be your advocates and safe space
- o Steps to take toward bringing resolution to your issue
- Come up with coping mechanisms and strategies to rise above your situation.
- In general work conflict, a professional can help you identify effective and productive conflict resolution techniques. They can identify places where you may have gone wrong.
- They can be your personal cheerleader, helping you to better see all of the good in your life.
- They can help you through any and all issues outside of this issue.
  - o Home life issues that could also be working against you
  - o Unresolved issues of your past work or home life that could be holding you back
  - o Helping you identify negative thought structures and inner workings that have held you back from your true potential

Overall, a professional can help you identify a pathway to a happier you, rising above your conflict, harassment, or bullying situation.

What to Look for in a Professional

Just like if you were trying to hire someone for an open position at work or someone to help with a home project, you want to consider several things that will help you find and hire a professional therapist. Below are key things to consider when looking for a professional.

Experience

You want to look at the number of years of experience and type of experience. You want to find someone who is known for helping someone in the areas that you need the most help with, whether that be conflict resolution, self-empowerment, assertiveness, emotional management, conflict resolution or all the above.

What Past Customers Have Said

As you would do when finding a good restaurant, hotel, or Airbnb, you want to look for someone who has had both a high number of ratings and high average rating. Someone who has twenty or more ratings and an average rating of 4.7 is better than a person with only three ratings and a 4.7. Additionally, you want to read any written reviews. Sometimes people give low reviews for things that would be trivial matters to you. And if someone has taken the time to write out a lengthy review, you can get a clear picture of both the pros and cons of working with that therapist.

Someone Who Vibes with You

Once you've landed on what appears to be two or three good therapists, you want to interview each of them as you would before hiring someone for any job. In addition to specific questions, you should ask the following general questions that will help you find the right therapist:

- What assessment will you use to baseline and measure progress in my situation?
- What is your philosophy and what methodology will you use to help me through my situation?

Most therapists will not be willing to go through an actual interview process, so you will likely have to schedule an initial session and essentially "interview" them at that session. There will be traits that you'll like in one therapist over the others. The following are some of the traits that you'll like or dislike that you would only know from having that first session/interview:

- What percentage of the time do they listen vs. talk?

- Do they pass the "vibe" test? Does their personality mesh well with your personality?
- Does it seem like this individual can help me with my specific situation?
- Will this person challenge me toward growth?
- Does this person bring positivity to my situation?
- Does it appear that unresolved issues of their personal past disproportionally affect their observations and advice?
- Is there any assessment tool they'll be using to baseline how your present situation is affecting you mentally and monitor for any change in the situation?
- The philosophy and type of counseling methodology they'll be using.

A professional can pretty much help you with everything I bring up in this book. If you purchased this book for yourself, then your situation is probably severe enough for you to need a professional for help.

Chapter 9 Homework

1. Answer yes or no to each of the following questions that were given at the beginning of this chapter:

   a. Do you regularly think of your work situation at home?

    b. Has your work situation caused you to lose sleep in the last month?

    c. Have you thought of getting a new job or explored other work in the last month because of your work situation?

    d. Do you feel your mental and/or physical well-being have been impacted by your situation?

    e. Is your work situation too much for you to bear alone?

2. If you answered "yes" to one or more of the above questions, look for a professional therapist or life coach to help you process your situation. Identify two professionals to interview.

3. Schedule one session with each of these professionals.

CHAPTER 10

PULLING IT ALL TOGETHER

Are you being bullied or harassed, or are you experiencing general work conflict? If you haven't already, take the bullying survey to answer this question. If you're getting more of a passive-aggressive form of bullying or harassment, it's going to be more difficult to point to one specific instance and say, "There it is." It's for this reason that bullies or harassers will choose this form.

If you're experiencing this type of bullying, look back over the list of covert forms of bullying in chapter 2. Check off items that apply in your situation. Of the twenty'six listed, how many did you check off? If you checked off more than five, then you're being bullied in this manner. Again, this can be the most damaging because it is the most difficult form for an organization to detect.

If you're able to point to specific instances of being bullied or harassed, then follow the steps of RECTIFY to attempt to bring resolution to your situation. The quicker you come to resolution, the quicker you'll get relief from the associated stress, freeing you up to be your creative, motivated, kick-ass self again. Quick and effective resolution to all forms of bullying, harassment, and conflict should not only matter to you—it should matter and be a priority for your organization and company.

Remember that you are more than what you do—you aren't a "human doing", you're a "human being". Separate yourself from what you do and look at your employment options from a completely different perspective. If you haven't made a pros and cons list of staying vs. leaving your current employer, do so now. Look at your workplace culture. Is the negative behavior that you're experiencing happening to others? Is the leadership of your organization ignoring or overlooking the negative behaviors in the organization? Are those who are raising issues being listened to or are they dismissed? If your bullying or harassment situation is a systemic problem occurring throughout your organization, then you should make your mental and physical well-being a priority and leave.

Remember and apply the power tools in the acronym EMPOWER. These tools can help lower the intensity of your feelings regarding your work situation and give you calm in the face of adversity.

- Exercise. Physical activity is not only an elixir for your physical fitness (making you stronger and healthier), it's elixir for your mental health, giving you the power to rise above your troubles. If physical activity isn't part of your daily routine, add it. You should be putting in at least a half hour workout per day, five days a week. Choose what you love to do because it will be easier to make it a habit. A class or group activity can give you the accountability you need to make exercise a habit, but individual exercise (like running or hiking) can be more meditative, allowing you the time and space to meditate on your work issues. Remember the example I shared—how my four-mile run one day gave me the clarity and creativity to change my work situation. This could happen to you too, giving you a clearer vision of your path forward. You too have options you haven't even thought of yet. There's a better path out there for you.

- Meditation. Remember that meditation, like physical fitness, can give you clarity in your situation. Meditation can give you peace during not only your work situation, but any storms in life that you may face. If you haven't made meditation a habit yet, do so. You should be spending at least five minutes a day meditating. For me, I set my phone timer for five minutes, clear my mind and use the techniques that I've learned and practiced over the years. If you haven't done this before, then buy a book on meditation or find a YouTube video on it. As with exercise, doing it the same time every day can help make it a habit. Join a meditation class to get accountability toward making it a habit—you'll probably get more accountability from an in-person course or class, but an online course will be more convenient.

- Positivity.
  - o Surround yourself with positivity. Lean into your positive relationships. If you haven't scheduled a time with one of your most positive friends or family members, do so.
  - o Be the positivity. You be the positive force that you would want to see in others. Being generous, kind, gentle, empathetic, loving, peaceful, and forgiving can help you rise above your situation. Put in at least one action in each of these areas.
  - o Affirmations. Remember that you are a badass! Start not only believing that but speaking that! There's power in our words and your words should reflect what you want your life to be. If you haven't started

daily affirmations yet, do so. You can pick affirmations from my list in chapter 6 or you can come up with your own. Speak these affirmations at least once a day until they become a daily habit. It's probably not a bad idea to line up your time for physical activity, your meditation, and your affirmations together.

- Off. Take time off for yourself daily and longer term. If you haven't scheduled a personal vacation, do so. The amount of time off that you take should be appropriate for your personal stress level from your given work conflict. If the stress level was/is significant enough, you should take time away from work.

- Welfare. Pay special attention to your personal health during this time by eating right, daily exercise, and good sleeping habits. If you've been tired from a poor night's sleep in the last week, try to determine the root cause why and use some of my chapter 6 suggestions to improve both the quality and duration of your sleep.

- Exhale. Do deep breathing exercises. If you haven't already, research and practice deep breathing exercises.

- Reverse. Flip the script on your bullying situation. See it as a growth opportunity for yourself or as an opportunity to change your career. You deserve better than your bullying or harassment situation because you're a badass. Remember that all of the greats had to first pass through the valley before getting to the mountaintop. Envision your mountaintop experience and then go out and climb it.

Create a safe space for yourself. Remember my example of the neighbor's cat coming onto our deck outside of the electric fence from the neighbor's dogs. If you haven't yet, find that safe space for yourself at your work and that remote place outside of work. Also, remember that you are your best advocate. Use your assertiveness techniques to respectfully stand up to your bullies or harassers to set up boundaries to protect yourself.

Training that can help. If you haven't done so yet, choose a personal development course that you think would best help you in your situation.

Finding a professional. If you haven't reached out to a professional, do so. Recall why it's imperative to get the help of a professional, as a professional will:

- More independently assess and evaluate your specific situation.
- Evaluate how the situation is affecting your mental and physical well-being.

- Come up with a plan of strategies and actions specific to resolving your situation.
- Come up with coping mechanisms and strategies to rise above your situation.
- In general work conflict, they can help you identify effective and productive conflict resolution techniques. They can identify places where you may have gone wrong, ultimately helping you in your path of personal improvement.
- They can be your personal cheerleader, helping you to better see all the good in your life.
- They can help you through all issues outside of this issue that could be contributing factors in your current conflicts at home and at work.
- Identify your path to a happier you by helping you see and understand your inner workings.

It's important for employees and organizations to have workplaces that are clear of all forms of harassment and bullying and have an organized functional approach to conflict resolution. Organizations that have employees who play well together will work well together.

Chapter 10 Homework

For some of my engineering courses in college, we were allowed a one-page "cheat sheet" of formulas and notes to help us take the test. Developing the cheat sheet forced me to go through the course material to find and write down the most pertinent equations and notes. The exercise of developing the cheat sheet was as helpful in preparing for a given test as having the cheat sheet. Develop a personal cheat sheet for key points and your actions from having read this book. At a minimum, your cheat sheet should include the following:

1. The three acronyms in the book (i.e., RECTIFY, PEACE, and EMPOWER) and the words associated with each letter in these acronyms.
2. Actions you plan on taking associated with each word in these acronyms.
3. If you've thought of leaving your current company, develop a pros and cons list for staying vs. leaving your current company.
4. Regarding creating "safe spaces" for yourself, identify a safe space at work and identify personal actions toward creating a safe space via self-advocacy.
5. Identify training for yourself now and two future courses.

This one-page cheat sheet is now your personal action plan for navigating and rising above your bullying situation.

www.ingramcontent.com/pod-product-compliance
Lightning Source LLC
Chambersburg PA
CBHW072308210326
41519CB00057B/3088